# THE ENTREPRENEUR'S GUIDE

## TO

D1795112

# MANAGING

# INTELLECTUAL

# PROPERTY

Paul E. Schaafsma

The Oasis Press® / PSI Research
Central Point, Oregon

Published by The Oasis Press

This publication is designed to provide accurate and authoritative information in regard
to the subject matter covered. It is sold with the understanding that the publisher is not
engaged in rendering legal, accounting, or other professional service. If legal advice or
other expert assistance is required, the services of a competent professional person
should be sought.
> *— from a declaration of principles jointly adopted by a committee of*
> *the American Bar Association and a committee of publishers.*

Editor: Gina Froelich
Managing Editor and Book Designer: Constance C. Dickinson
Compositor: Jan Olsson
Cover and Illustration Designer: J. C. Young

Please direct any comments, questions, or suggestions regarding this book to
The Oasis Press®/PSI Research:

> Editorial Department
> P.O. Box 3727
> Central Point, OR 97502
> (541) 245-6502
> (541) 245-6505 *fax*
> info@psi-research.com *e-mail*


The Oasis Press® is a Registered Trademark of Publishing Services, Inc.,
an Oregon corporation doing business as PSI Research.

Schaafsma, Paul E., 1960–
        The entrepreneur's guide to managing intellectual property / Paul E. Schaafsma.
                p.   cm.
        Includes bibliographical references and index.
        ISBN 1-55571-617-2
        1. Intellectual property—Economic aspects—United States.  I. Title.

KF2979 .S33 2001
346.7304'8—dc21                                                    2001034359

Printed in the United States of America
First Edition 10 9 8 7 6 5 4 3 2 1

 Printed on recycled paper when available.

# TABLE OF CONTENTS

# PREFACE

With the door to the U.S. Patent Office now open to Internet entrepreneurs, the importance of the rights that protect intangible assets has never been greater. However, these intellectual property rights involve complex, obscure principles, which makes understanding — let alone managing — intellectual property assets challenging.

This book effectively bridges the gap between attorneys who understand the law and managers who are called upon to make business decisions regarding intellectual property assets. The chapters that follow succinctly explain intellectual property in the language of business. Case studies demonstrate real-world examples to bring these rights to life. However, this book is in no way intended to make patent attorneys out of managers. The practice of patent law is a full-time profession that should be left to the professionals. Rather, this book provides managers with insight into principles that can be used in more effectively managing intellectual property. With this insight, managers can become entrepreneurial managers of intellectual property.

The concept of the entrepreneurial management of intellectual property does not depend on the size of an enterprise. It does not depend on the phase of the development of the company, although startups may well not survive without entrepreneurial management. The principles that follow can be applied by any size company at any stage of development to better manage intellectual property. Moreover, investment managers such as venture capitalists can apply these principles to better allocate research and development funding.

Likewise, the concept of the entrepreneurial management of intellectual property does not depend on the type of technology used, although given the recent emergence of e-commerce patent rights and the recent decline in the NASDAQ index, dotcoms may well not survive without entrepreneurial management. These principles can be applied to any type of technology, ranging from e-commerce to biotechnology.

Entrepreneurial management of intellectual property is about more effectively managing intellectual property assets. This results in two benefits to the company:

- ▶ First, entrepreneurial management of intellectual property means better decision making that results in stronger, more significant, and more defendable intellectual property, which secures to the entrepreneurial company a privileged place in the market.
- ▶ Second, entrepreneurial management of intellectual property means spending resources more intelligently in managing intellectual property, thereby preserving the corporation's resources for other uses, like new product development.

In a nutshell, the entrepreneurial management of intellectual property is about managing limited resources more intelligently to get more bang for the company's intellectual property buck. Companies that delegate these strategic decisions to the company's intellectual property attorneys cannot be entrepreneurial managers of intellectual property. Likewise, managers who rely on simplistic guides to gauge the strength of their intellectual property, such as counting the number of patents and filings, or reciting the number of times patents are cited in subsequent patent filings, cannot be entrepreneurial managers of intellectual property. Nor can managers who simply profess clichés like, "we are strategically managing our intellectual property" or "we aggressively protect all of our innovations" be entrepreneurial managers of intellectual property.

The entrepreneurial management of intellectual property is accomplished by managers who are willing to familiarize themselves with this complex area, not just in the economics and finances of intellectual property, but also in the law. The entrepreneurial management of intellectual property is accomplished by managers who know these decisions affect their personal assets, and consequently are willing to commit their personal time to educate themselves, regardless of who actually foots the bill.

# PATENTS AND E-COMMERCE

In 1998, a federal appellate court ruled that a financial service algorithm (a step-by-step computer process) that moved electronic funds was patentable subject matter. More recently: Priceline.com sued Microsoft's travel web site, operated by Expedia.com, for infringement of its U.S. Patent No. 5,794,207 directed towards online "reverse auctions"; Amazon.com sued barnesandnoble.com for infringement of its U.S. Patent No. 5,960,411 directed to "one-click" ordering; and an individual sued Yahoo! for infringement of her U.S. Patent No. 5,895,454 directed to online shopping carts.

All these events have been widely reported in the business press, and this publicity has awakened entrepreneurs to the applicability of patents to electronic commerce. Despite this recent focus, these events are not the result of a change in the applicability of patents to e-commerce. For example, the patent directed towards online shopping technology was filed in April 1997, the patent owned by Amazon. com was filed in September 1997, and the patent owned by Priceline.com was filed in September 1996. Indeed, U.S. Patent No. 5,193,056, the patent that was the subject of the federal appellate court's ruling, was filed in March 1991 and issued in March 1993. Moreover, the ruling did little to change the state of the law — software that moves electronic funds has long satisfied the standard for patentable subject matter.

These events have sparked intense debate in both the legal and the Internet communities about whether patents should apply to innovation on the Internet. "The application of patents to our emerging industry is unprecedented," cry the critics. "It will stifle innovation." In response, some ignore the applicability of patents to the e-commerce industry. However, those who hope these issues disappear from the e-commerce landscape should remember the experience of the biotechnology industry. In the infancy of that industry, the courts resoundingly affirmed the even more troublesome question of patenting life.

Which is not to say all e-commerce patents will withstand the inevitable attacks. In addition to patentable subject matter, an invention must represent an advance in the state of the technology to be entitled to a patent. Even the federal appellate court decision largely responsible for the recent publicity did not pass judgment on the obviousness of the technology — the ruling was limited to whether a financial service algorithm that moved electronic funds qualified as patentable subject matter. The proverbial jury is still out on whether the current wave of patents that put existing paradigms of business in electronic format will ultimately withstand attack.

Beyond lacking the requisite technological advance, e-commerce patents could be particularly susceptible from another angle of attack. A patent must sufficiently describe the technology to enable it to be replicated without undue trouble. While line-by-line source code is not required to meet this standard, the dearth of technological explanation accompanying many e-commerce paper patents is troubling. For example, the patent directed towards online shopping carts which forms the basis of the lawsuit filed against Yahoo! uses about 225 words to describe the technology. In contrast, Priceline.com's patent directed towards online "reverse auctions" has more than 1,200 words describing its technology.

This uncertainty requires that entrepreneurial managers of e-commerce be particularly sophisticated in managing intellectual property. In exploring the entrepreneurial management of intellectual property, we follow the progression of George Marvin as he struggles to get his startup business running. Because e-commerce managers can learn much about the entrepreneurial management of intellectual property from those businesses in which intellectual property has long been a factor, we look to George's startup audio speaker business as our ongoing case study.[1]

## Meet George Marvin, Would-Be Entrepreneurial Manager

George Marvin felt out of place as he admired the view from the waiting room of the prestigious law firm. He contrasted the view with the view of the parking lot from his new company. George knew the office space in which he sat did not come cheaply. While the stately marble facade represented power and success to the passing businesspeople in their $1,000 suits, George could ill afford the resources large companies expend in managing their intellectual property. It was not that he considered these lawyers and businesspeople to be his intellectual superiors; with an undergraduate degree in engineering from Purdue University and a M.B.A. from Northwestern University's Kellogg Graduate School of Business, George was not intimidated. Rather, his concern arose from the startup status of his company.

George, his wife Mildred Marvin, a marketing whiz whom he met while at Kellogg, and Chip Norton, George's technical wizard, recently set up a company, tentatively named Marvin Enterprises. The three entrepreneurs raised $100,000 from savings, friends, and family to fund Marvin Enterprises. Marvin Enterprises was formed to develop and commercialize a new audio speaker system they code-named the "gargle-blaster." The gargle-blaster system uses sophisticated digital compression software to allow significant miniaturization of audio speakers while retaining an extremely high quality of sound. George Marvin was the first to see the potential of such digital compression software in the speaker industry.

The speaker industry includes more than 300 speaker brands competing for a $2 billion (in sales) market. The two largest companies, Bose and JBL, each have about ten percent of the market, or about $200 million each in sales. This leaves about 290 brands battling for the remaining 80 percent, with each having an average market share of one-fourth of one percent and average sales of about $5 million.

Assuming a relatively short product life cycle of five years in consumer electronics and also assuming two years to get Marvin Enterprises' speakers to market, George has used high-risk valuation principles favored by venture capitalists to calculate a value for Marvin Enterprises. At this startup stage, the certainty of future cash flows based on future sales of the gargle-blaster speakers is risky. Venture capitalists estimate that out of every six ventures in which they invest, two will fail, two will succeed, and two will join the "living dead," with sufficient sales to survive but not prosper. Because of these factors, venture capitalists use a 40 percent discount rate for net present valuation. Assuming the gargle-blaster speakers gain a market share of one percent and average sales of about $20 million, George conservatively applied a discount rate of 50 percent to value Marvin Enterprises at $15 million.

To arrive at even this discount rate, George, Mildred, and Chip performed extensive business due diligence on competitive products in the marketplace, customers' needs and expectations, price elasticity of demand, costs of goods sold, and distribution channels. In addition, George retained advisors in areas in which George, Mildred, and Chip weren't strong in order to ensure, for example, that distribution channels were realistic, his cost-of-goods sold was achievable, his valuation model was financially sound, and his market was identifiable and targetable. George was now at the law firm to discuss intellectual property issues facing introduction of the gargle-blaster speakers.

Despite tentatively naming his company Marvin Enterprises, George had already begun to rethink this naming strategy. Will he use the name of the company as the name of the products? Does George wish to develop a distinctive name for more than one product across a product line? Do our entrepreneurs wish to designate individual products within the product line by a generic name, a numerical designation, or even a descriptive name? Do they wish to develop a family of marks that share a common feature that can be used to build on previously established consumer recognition?

Once an appropriate strategy is chosen, steps should be taken to minimize the likelihood of future conflicts with other businesses. Often, the only due diligence to which a proposed name is exposed is calling a secretary of state's office or linking to the Network Solutions website — *http://www.networksolutions.com/cgibin/whois/ whois* — to check whether the name has been taken. Unfortunately, this inquiry only exposes conflicts when someone is using exactly the same name. Names for similar businesses that are similar in sound, meaning, or appearance will not be identified and may very well result in a future conflict over the use of the name.

If the strategy in choosing a company name is to convey to consumers a message about the company, descriptive names are often chosen. However, descriptive names involve two distinct, apparently conflicting drawbacks. First, the user of a descriptive name may not be able to stop competitors from using similar names. Second, the user may be prohibited from using a descriptive name in a product-line expansion if someone else is using the name.

This apparent contradiction arises from the treatment of descriptive terms under the law. Use of a descriptive name does not automatically entitle exclusive trademark rights; thus, competitors may be able to use uncomfortably similar names. However, if a descriptive name is used as a trademark for an unchallenged period it can evolve over time into a protectable trademark; thus, competitors may have rights in that name in an area of product-line expansion. While these factors do not necessarily rule out choosing a descriptive name, that choice carries implications that entrepreneurial managers should understand in making branding decisions.

In addition to branding strategies, other forms of intellectual property protection should be considered. Prior to returning to business school, George worked for a large consumer electronics company. At this company, he played a role in several acquisitions of startups. In what his company paid for these startups, George saw first-hand the value of patents. Utility patents protect technological developments with a government-sponsored, 20-year period of exclusive use of the new technology. Classic examples include protection given to a new or improved drug, an improved anti-lock braking system, or a new recording medium. Patents are drafted and negotiated with the government by patent attorneys who specialize in this area of the law.

George understood patents are often the only barrier standing between his startup and the established consumer electronic corporations against which he will compete. Without patents, these competitors could simply wait to see if Marvin

Enterprises' new product was successful. If it was, they could reverse engineer and sell competing speakers without having incurred either the research and development costs or Marvin Enterprises' risk of new product introduction.

Because Marvin Enterprises' use of the gargle-blaster system combined several technological advances, George anticipated he would need as many as four separate patent applications. With an electronics patent application requiring from 40 to 60 hours of legal work in addition to the time George and Chip Norton spend explaining the technology to the patent attorney, each application could easily cost $10,000 in legal fees alone. Despite this cost, George knew it was worth it; $35,000 of the friends' and families' financing was budgeted to this cause.

Later in the company's development, George would assess the future direction of the company. He had chosen the lowest-lying fruit for his initial efforts. Like many emerging companies, George's business plan included well-thought-out product expansion into related areas. While admittedly the chance of great success in these areas was a long shot, George was dismayed at the degree to which the venture capitalists discount the potential of these markets. George was determined to make some of these areas pay off, although they were not his initial focus.

Finally, George had not given much thought to his end game. While visions of initial public offerings danced in his head, other strategies to cash out also might be available. Could acquiring a strategic partner add value to his enterprise? Could technology be licensed, either inwardly to develop new products or outwardly to gain revenues from noncompeting uses? The decisions George would soon make in managing his intellectual property would affect his options for the future direction of his company.

## Startup Technical Due Diligence

George was at the law firm to discuss the intellectual property issues facing his introduction of the gargle-blaster speaker. However, by waiting this long in the product development cycle to consult with an attorney, George was already acting decidedly nonentrepreneurial.

George had performed extensive business due diligence but he had not performed intellectual property due diligence. In nonentrepreneurial companies, the risks of conflicts with competitors' intellectual property are left to chance. To entrepreneurially manage Marvin Enterprises' intellectual property, legal due diligence should have come early in the product development cycle to better understand the proprietary rights landscape. New-product legal due diligence consists of three areas:

- ► technology due diligence,
- ► trademark due diligence (see Chapter 3), and
- ► copyright due diligence (see Chapter 4).

## Three Stages of Due Diligence

As with any type of due diligence, entrepreneurial managers understand that no amount of depth can completely eliminate risk. For example, the confidential nature of many pending patent applications means applications in the pipeline to issue as patents in the future cannot be reviewed. Like all due diligence, the art of intellectual property due diligence lies in properly assessing the cost/benefit tradeoffs on a case-by-case analysis.

Essentially, new-product technical due diligence entails three stages:

- ▶ Is title to the technology clearly in the company?
- ▶ Does exploitation of the technology infringe on any third party rights?
- ▶ What is the potential value of the intellectual property?

Depending on the nature of the technology, all, none, or some of these stages are appropriate. Additionally, because most intellectual property extends only within national boundaries, legal due diligence should be considered for each country where a significant market for the technology is expected.

Even prior to stage one due diligence, steps should have been taken to ensure title to the technology resides in the company. Anyone involved with the creation of the technology should be under a written, contractual obligation (an employment agreement or consulting agreement) to assign their rights to the company.

**Stage One Due Diligence**

If the company does not own the technology, but has accessed rights by license, an understanding of the licensed rights is essential. The barrier to entry — the hindrance to competitors — such license provides varies from an exclusive licensee, which is tantamount to ownership, to nonexclusive. The financial impact of any royalty payments should be included as an additional cost-of-goods sold. Finally, any limitations placed in the licensed rights — such as a limited field of use license — should be understood, particularly if the company plans on extending the technology beyond the current product line.

If a significant portion of the technology is trade secret, special issues arise. To maintain information as trade secret, reasonable steps must be taken to keep the information confidential. For example, employment agreements, workplace security, and agreements requiring confidential treatment from third parties — such as suppliers and distributors — should be in place.

Stage two due diligence focuses on whether exploitation of the technology infringes third party rights. Just as the owner of real property does not necessarily have the right to any use of that property — due to, for example, zoning and environmental laws — the patent grants the patent owner no affirmative right to commercialize the technology if it infringes third party rights. Chapters 2 and 7 explain these principles in detail. Particularly before embarking on a significant investment of resources in developing new products, some level of due diligence is advisable.

**Stage Two Due Diligence**

**Stage Three
Due
Diligence**

In stage three due diligence, the scope of any patents that protect the new technology should be understood. Understanding the scope of patents allows entrepreneurial managers to better predict the level of competition from economic substitute products. This information is helpful in business decisions such as pricing strategies and marketplace penetration. The state of the technological art upon which the technology improves should be surveyed to understand the significance of the innovation. The economic valuation of patents described in Chapter 5 is important to intuitively understanding this issue. The technique of patent charting described in Chapter 6 represents a particularly efficient way for entrepreneurial managers to gain this intuitive understanding.

## Whose Technology Is It Anyway?

**CASE
STUDY**

Until the introduction of the IBM personal computer in August 1981, the world of personal computing was largely made up of a group of fanatical computer hobbyists. Stephen Wozniak and Steven Jobs were two of the most fanatical. In 1970 Stephen "Woz" Wozniak was attending college. The following year he started working in a computer shop in Southern California. Because of his interest in computers, he didn't return to college. In 1973 he met Steven Jobs, who was working for Hewlett-Packard in a summer job. Like Wozniak, Jobs attended college, didn't like it, and quit. Wozniak and Jobs worked together to create an arcade game for Atari. Later, Wozniak designed a "blue box," which allowed the user to make free illegal long distance telephone calls. Jobs helped Wozniak sell these blue boxes.

In 1974, Jobs worked for Atari as a programmer to save money for a trip to India to find spiritual enlightenment. When he returned, he joined "Woz" at the Homebrew Computer Club, a group of computer hobbyists who met weekly to discuss the latest in personal computing. He convinced Wozniak to design a small computer for personal use. In April 1976, Jobs and Wozniak founded Apple Computer in Palo Alto, California. Wozniak bought a microprocessor for $20 and in their now-famous garage, built a computer around it. They named it the Apple I. In fact, the Apple I was little more than a circuit board.

In 1977, Wozniak built a second-generation computer that could be directly connected into a television. They named it the Apple II. From 1977 to 1978, Wozniak designed a floppy-disk drive for the computer. In 1978, Apple moved from Palo Alto to Cupertino, California. In 1979, Apple visited Xerox's Research Center in Palo Alto. There they saw a presentation of an impressive array of computer innovations.

Xerox's Palo Alto Research Center is better know as PARC. Formed in 1970, over the next decade PARC was responsible for an amazing number of cutting-edge computer innovations, including: the laser printer, PARC's only successful commercial product; the Ethernet; the first desktop computer, known as the Alto; and the first portable computer, the Notetaker.

In the middle of the seventies, PARC developed a computer operating system that allowed the user to interact with the computer through the use of a small, hand-held device. Another research project in the late seventies used fanciful visual displays and graphical images to aid user interaction with the computer. Xerox's complex integrated office system, which included these innovations, was introduced in 1981 as the Star Workstation. This expensive system, however, was made obsolete by Apple and IBM even before it was introduced.

In December 1979, Steven Jobs and a team of Apple programmers gained exposure to these Xerox corporate gems. By then the Apple II was on the market which, when combined with the first "killer app" — the VisiCalc spreadsheet — was the first legitimate personal business computer. Apple was developing the next generation of personal computers, to be introduced under the brand name LISA. In exchange for an investment stake in Apple before its initial public offering, Xerox's corporate headquarters agreed to demonstrate PARC's technology to Jobs.

In 1983, Apple introduced the LISA. This personal computer allowed the user to interact with the computer through the use of a small, handheld device dubbed a "mouse," and included fanciful visual displays and graphical images to aid user interaction with the computer. While LISA was a commercial flop, Apple quickly introduced the successful Macintosh personal computer. The Macintosh likewise used a mouse and fanciful visual displays and graphical images. Four years later, Microsoft introduced an operating system for IBM-compatible computers that used fanciful visual displays and graphical images to aid user interaction with the computer, dubbed Windows. Now several companies were using similar operating systems for which the ownership was not clear, and the inevitable lawsuits followed.

Apple sued Microsoft, claiming Apple's copyrights were infringed by the Windows graphical user interface. Xerox sued Apple, claiming Apple misappropriated the graphical user interface. In the context of Xerox's willing demonstration of the technology to Apple, Apple's exposure of the technology at Xerox, and Apple's charge against Microsoft, clear proprietary ownership of this technology was lacking. The court threw up its hands and dismissed these claims. One can only wonder what Caribbean island the stockholders of Xerox would own if these corporate gems had been better protected.

————————

**CASE STUDY** CONT.

## Endnote

1. This hypothetical case study is loosely based on the venture capital case study found in Chapter 15 of Richard Brealey & Stewart Myers, *Principles of Corporate Finance* (4th Ed. 1981).

## CHAPTER 1

# ECONOMIC DEVELOPMENT

**The**

**Value of**

**Patents**

While at a large consumer electronics company, George recognized the value of patents. However, he had not considered the significance of what the government was offering with patents — a government-sponsored economic "monopoly" on his gargle-blaster speaker technology. Nor had he contemplated the government-sponsored prohibition against copying his software code or the government-sponsored prohibition against palming off his branding decisions. As a first step on the journey to better understand intellectual property from a business perspective, it is important for entrepreneurial managers to understand how these extraordinary rights grew into existence.

## The Italian City-States and the Guilds

The earliest examples of such exclusive rights are found in the Italian city-states of the fifteenth century. In this period, skilled artisans formed guilds as a way to gain political power. Guilds often negotiated from the city-states the power to control membership. To identify the origin of sanctioned goods, guilds imprinted marks on goods made by the guild members. The use of these marks as identifiers of a guild's products originated trademark rights.

The guilds also regulated disputes between members. This dispute resolution grew into formal rules of the guild. For example, an early silk manufacturers' guild in the city-state of Genoa granted members who designed new patterns the exclusive right to make their patterns.[1] In 1474, the woolen manufacturer's guild in the city-state of Florence barred copying of the pattern of a member.[2] As the prohibition against copying patterns was developing, the interest of publishers in controlling the production of books was also developing. The regulation of guild members' designs and book publishing originated copyrights.

As the guild rules grew out of dispute resolution among its members, the exclusive rights granted by guilds focused on use of the guild's mark and copying of members' patterns or designs. Unlike patents, which developed as a tool of economic development, copyright protection and trademark rights originated from a "natural rights" theory of protection. This philosophical difference continues to this day, with patents best viewed as a tool of economic development, copyrights best understood as a prohibition against plagiarism, and the unfair competition laws best characterized as consumer protection laws.

## Exclusive Rights

The next step in the development of intellectual property was the use of exclusive rights as tools to encourage economic progress. While initially used in order to encourage the migration of artisans who were skilled in areas in which a city-state was lacking, soon the city-states recognized the usefulness of these grants of exclusivity to promote innovation. Thus, the grant of exclusive rights to investors, which evolved into patents, originated as a tool for economic development. To a large extent, however, the city-states' use of exclusive rights in this way was a threat to the power and prestige of a guild. For example, if an invention made a guild's existing technology obsolete, the grant of exclusivity to use the new technology could obsolete the guild. As a result, power began to transfer from the guilds to the government of the city-states.

An example of an early use of such exclusive rights involving a guild occurred in 1406 in the city-state of Florence. At the time, the art of mounting steel-wire bristles was unknown in Florence. Guerimus de Mera, a resident of Milan where this art was highly developed, responded to an offer of ten years of tax exemption to introduce the art to Florence. After demonstrating his process of mounting steel-wire bristles, he entered into a contract with the Woolens Guild of Florence to exercise and teach the art, with the understanding that those he taught would not use it independently for a time. In 1409, the city-state of Florence issued a decree approving the contract.

By the time these exclusive rights evolved into grants for innovation, the guilds' involvement was virtually gone. The earliest grant of an exclusive right for an invention can be traced to 1421, when the city-state of Florence granted the exclusive right to a barge that the architect Filippo Brunelleschi designed.[3] (See Case Study: Brunelleschi – the First Patentee, below.) The first example of a broader policy to encourage innovation occurred around 1474, when the city-state of Venice passed a law that broadly granted exclusivity to the inventor of a machine or process.[4] This law provided for destruction of infringing devices and payment of a fee to the inventor. Under this law, in 1594 a 20-year term of exclusivity was granted to the inventor of a "machine for raising water and irrigating land with small expense and great convenience." The inventor was Galileo Galilei.[5]

## Brunelleschi – the First Patentee

❖

CASE

STUDY

❖

Filippo Brunelleschi was born in 1377 in the Italian city-state of Florence. Guilds were prominent in this postfeudal society. Filippo's father belonged to the Guild of the Lawyers and Judges, which placed the Brunelleschi family in the upper class of Florence society. Other major guilds included the Guild of the Merchants and Industrialists, the Bankers Guild, the Woolens Guild, the Silk Guild, the Furriers Guild, and the Pharmacists Guild. As was the custom at the time, blacksmiths, carpenters, masons, and bakers formed lesser guilds. These guilds fought over and divided up markets and maintained their trade secrets. The guilds also held great political power. Of the nine seats on the Supreme Council of State, seven were reserved for the major guilds.

Early in his adulthood, Brunelleschi joined the Silk Guild and became a goldsmith. There he also became a watchmaker, learning about the mechanics of motion. He learned to shape bronze, wood, and stone, which evolved into an interest in architecture. By 1404, he was a consultant to the committee in charge of important public building programs.

Between 1420 and 1432, Brunelleschi designed a dome for the great cathedral in Florence. He encountered three significant technological hurdles in building the dome: how to rapidly deliver materials to the building site; how to raise the materials to the level of the dome; and how to support the materials in place while building. He raised the materials through a system of winches and gears driven by oxen. To support the materials, he rejected the use of rigid wooden centering that builders had previously used. Instead, he devised scaffolds that enabled workers on each of the eight sides of the dome to work on the same level simultaneously.

It was Brunelleschi's solution to the difficulties in delivering materials to the building site that was the subject of the first patent. Florence lies 145 feet above sea level and 50 miles inland, with the Arno River connecting Florence with the sea. The Arno is shallow, allowing navigation only by small boats, particularly during the dry season. Brunelleschi designed a ship to overcome these difficulties. He called his boat *Badalone*, which means "monster."

The exclusive grant from the city-state of Florence describes the problems *Badalone* was designed to address.

> FILIPPO BRUNELLESCHI ... has invented some machine or kind of ship, by means of which he thinks he can easily, at any time, bring in merchandise and load on the river Arno ....[6]

Dispensing with any definition of the scope of his exclusivity, Brunelleschi's rights were broadly expressed.

> ... [N]o person ... shall dare or presume, within three years ... (a) to have, hold, or use in any manner, be it newly invented or made in new form, a machine or ship or other instrument designed to import or ship or transport on water any merchandise or any things or goods, except such ship or machine or instrument as they may have used until now for similar operations, or (b) to ship or transport or to have shipped or transported any merchandise or goods on other ships, machines, or instruments for water transport than were familiar and usual until now; and further that any such new or newly shaped machine etc. shall be burned.[7]

Thus, others were prohibited not just from using Brunelleschi's design of *Badalone* but also from using any new design "except such ship or machine or instrument as they may have used until now for similar operations."[8]

Unfortunately for Brunelleschi, like many later patents, it appears his invention was a commercial flop. In June 1427, a purchase order for "100 florentine Tons" (37.5 short tons) of white marble "to be shipped by Brunelleschi" was issued.[9] In May 1428, a book entry required Brunelleschi to ship "by small boats" the quantity of white marble he shipped from the City of Pisa on the coast to "the castle in Empoli and Castelfranco by the *Badalone*."[10] It appears *Badalone* never made it to Florence; Empoli is located between the coast and Florence. No record of a later voyage of *Badalone* exists.

Fortunately for Brunelleschi, his subsequent inventions were considerably more successful. He died in 1446, having achieved considerable fame as an inventor and architect and is buried under his dome in the great cathedral in Florence. The epitaph on his tomb reads:

> What Filippo the architect did in Daedalus' art [invention], not only the wonders of this celebrated temple witness it, but it is documented by various machines invented by him with divine ingeniousness.[11]

CASE STUDY

CONT.

## The Scholastic Economic Period

The widespread use of exclusive rights to encourage economic activity developed concurrently in several areas of Western Europe near the end of the sixteenth century. This is the same period when general economic thought was evolving beyond the ethical and philosophical focus of the Scholastic economic period. Prior to the seventeenth century, Western Europe consisted of feudal societies, with the major economic focus on subsistence agriculture. Society was divided into serfs, landlords, royalty, and the church. The relationships among these groups were dictated less by economic relations than by historical tradition. During this period, what little economic theory that developed did so in the context of the ethical and philosophical thought of the time.

The focus by Scholastic writers such as St. Thomas Aquinas was not on economic growth, but rather on guidelines for economic relationships based on notions of religious fairness. Aquinas, for example, justified private ownership of property according to biblical guidelines.[12] As the end of the sixteenth century approached, feudal society underwent an economic transformation. Improvements in agrarian and industrial technology disrupted the division of labor. Mechanical power from water and wind replaced man and animal power. The feudal system gave way to the increasing influence and authority of the city-state.

## Mercantilism

This changing society also gave rise to new levels of economic thought. Merchants urged policies to encourage economic growth. This period is known as the Mercantilism period. Thomas Mun, a director of England's East India Company, is an example of an influential Mercantilist. Not surprisingly, given his interest in the East India Company, Mun's writings encouraged importation to England of raw materials and exportation from England of manufactured goods. This resulted in an accumulation of precious metals such as gold and silver in England.[13]

Mun's view was based on the erroneous assumption that the earth's riches were limited, and that by importing raw materials and exporting manufactured goods, a nation received a larger proportion of the earth's riches. This view has been discredited by modern economic thought, under which trade increases the earth's riches to the benefit of all trading partners.

Like Mun's writings, much of Mercantilist thought was designed to promote the self-interests of the merchants who exposed it. Thus, the use of governmental grants of exclusivity to encourage economic development arose at a time when merchants were advocating economic principles designed to support their self-interest. Unlike most Mercantilist thought, which the advent of Classical economics in the eighteenth century discredited, use of limited grants of exclusivity to encourage economic development remains a viable tool of economic growth.

Governments grant an economic monopoly on technology to financially encourage innovation. While the attraction of individual creativity into innovation is important, the attraction of financial resources to support commercialization of innovation is at least equally important. The potential economic reward during the period of exclusivity is the carrot that attracts investment into innovation.[14]

A financial incentive for innovation is easy to justify if an economy without patents is imagined. Competitors could freely reverse engineer and copy successful innovative products that were developed at substantial cost. Not only would these competitors avoid the research and development costs of the innovator, they could also avoid the high risk of new product introduction by picking and choosing successful products. Against this backdrop, what firm would expend research funds? What venture capitalist would back an emerging company against a large, entrenched competitor? Product innovation would evaporate and society would lose the benefit of new innovator.

## The Statute of Monopolies

With the grant of such privileged economic position comes the potential for corruption. In England, where U.S. law originated, the granting of exclusive rights was a privilege of the Crown. The use of this privilege originally encouraged regional economic development. In 1326, Edward III developed a policy of encouraging the importation of useful technologies. For example, in 1331 an English letter of protection was granted to Flemish weavers.[15] In 1440 a similar letter of protection was granted to the inventor of a process for manufacturing salt.[16] Usually such grants included requirements to train apprentices.

Unfortunately, royalty such as Elizabeth I and James I used the Crown's privilege to bestow special favors on political friends and relatives, rather than to encourage economic growth. Elizabeth and James' use of grants to protect illegitimate monopolies resulted in price inflation that led to public discontent. After several promises of reform were broken, the discontent led to the passage of the Statute of Monopolies in 1624.

Better understood as an anti-monopoly statute, the Statute of Monopolies generally prohibited the Crown from granting monopolies. The Statute contained certain exceptions to the prohibition against monopolies, including use of exclusive rights as a reward for the introduction of new technologies.[17] After some conflict between the Crown and Parliament, the Statute of Monopolies was ultimately successful in curbing abuses, although the grant of an exclusive right to inventors remained subject to the Crown's discretion. English common law after 1623 developed the concept of a specification that described how to replicate the invention and combinations of preexisting technology to judge the novelty of an invention, concepts that remain in use today.

Likewise, interested parties such as authors challenged publishers' early control over printed works. In 1710, the Statute of Anne was passed which, like the Statute of Monopolies, limited the rights of publishers.

## The New World

In the New World, most of the English colonies provided for limited terms of exclusivity to encourage economic development. Like the early use of such grants in England and Italy, the early use in the colonies focused on importation of useful arts into the developing colonies, although grants to inventors also occurred. Because of the abuses in England, most colonial grants were free of the discretion that gave rise to the Statue of Monopolies.

By the time the United States Constitution was drafted in 1789,[18] patents had been used to induce economic growth for over 300 years. Indeed, in his seminal work about free markets published in 1776, Adam Smith recognized the value of patents in encouraging innovation as an established form of economic development.[19] By 1790, when the Congress passed the first Patent Act, use of patents to reward innovation and encourage economic growth was well established in Western economic and legal thought. By legislative standards, the Patent Act of 1790 has remained remarkably intact for more than 200 years.

## Asian Cultures

Those considering the development of intellectual property in the Pacific Rim should be mindful of this lengthy development of intellectual property in Western economic and legal culture. Western economic and legal thought has had over 500 years to refine intellectual property. While increasingly recognizing the usefulness of intellectual property as a tool for economic growth, Asian cultures lack the experience of Western countries in intellectual property. This lack of experience combined with the communal cultural focus in much of Asia helps explain the reluctance of such countries to embrace Western-style intellectual property.

## Endnotes

1. Frank D. Prager, "The Early Growth and Influence of Intellectual Property," *Journal of the Patent and Trademark Office Society (JPTOS)* 34 (Feb. 1952): 106, 112.
2. Ibid.
3. Frank D. Prager, "Brunelleschi's Patent," *JPTOS* 28 (Feb. 1946): 109.
4. Prager, "Early Growth," 130.
5. P. J. Frederico, "Origins and Early History of Patents," *JPTOS* 11 (1929): 304.
6. Prager, "Brunelleschi's Patent," 109.
7. Ibid.
8. Ibid.
9. Ibid., 124.
10. Ibid.
11. Ibid., 120.
12. St. Thomas Aquinas, *Summa Theologica* (c. 1273), I-II, Q. 94, art. 5.
13. Thomas Mun, *A Discourse of Trade from England unto the East Indies* (1621); and *England's Treasure by Foreign Trade* (1628).
14. *King Instruments Corp. v. Perego*, 65 F. 3d 941 (Fed. Cir. 1995).
15. Ibid. 293.
16. Ibid.
17. 21 King James c3 (1623).
18. "The Congress shall have Power ... to promote the progress of Science and useful Arts, by securing for limited times to Authors and Inventors the exclusive right to their respective writings and discoveries ...." U.S. Const. art. I, §8, cl. 8.
19. Adam Smith, *An Inquiry into the Nature and Causes of the Wealth of Nations*, bk. V, ch. 1, (1776 Cannan ed.), 712.

## CHAPTER 2

# PATENT FUNDAMENTALS

**What**

**Is a**

**Patent?**

Having played a role in several acquisitions of startups before returning to business school, George understood patents were the only barriers between his startup and the established consumer electronic corporations against which he would compete. Without patents, these competitors could simply sit back and wait to see if Marvin Enterprises' new product was successful. If it was, they could reverse engineer and sell it, incurring neither Marvin Enterprises' research and development costs nor its risk of new product introduction. (For a description of the process and costs of filing a patent application, see Appendix A.)

George also understood the need to manage intellectual property as he managed his company's finance and marketing. To entrepreneurially manage his company's intellectual property, he had to take an active role in strategic decision making, taking advice from the experts but ultimately making the decisions himself. To entrepreneurially manage his company's intellectual property, he needed a basic understanding of the patent ground rules. Thus, while at business school he tightened his belt, had an extra cup of coffee, and signed up for a course on intellectual property.

Nevertheless, George waited too long before he thought to investigate patent protection for the gargle-blaster. The project had been underway for months and discussion about market introduction was beginning. A meeting was called to discuss this issue, a rough prototype of the design was on the conference room table, and patents were finally mentioned for the first time.

> Mildred Marvin (examining prototype): This thing does not work anything like we discussed at our last design meeting!
>
> Chip Norton (impatiently): I told you at the design review meeting that I could only put a rough prototype together for this meeting. Those are only small kinks, which I will work out later.
>
> George: Ladies and gentlemen, let's get started. At our last meeting, engineering gave me a rundown of where we stand in the product development. I believe we are sufficiently close to completion that we need to start to develop a strategy for introducing this product. For example, if this product is as successful as we all anticipate, what can we do to prevent the scum at XYZ Competitor Corporation from stealing our idea?
>
> Chip: Well, last week we called a patent attorney. She's initiating a patentability search, but my fear is the scope of this patent would be somewhat narrow and would not preclude competitive products altogether. Knowing that a patent is one of the few things standing between us and those lowlifes at XYZ, we'll undoubtedly spend the money and file the patent application, which will at least slow them down and hopefully mean their product will be somewhat inferior to ours.
>
> George: Good. That will hopefully provide some protection against XYZ's copying.

While many details of patents are best left to lawyers, to entrepreneurially manage intellectual property the basics of patent law should be understood. A patent is the only form of intellectual property that prevents duplication of the basic functionality of a product. While valuable in serving as an identifier of the source of a product and protecting the reputation associated with that product, a trademark will not prevent replication of the product itself. Likewise, a copyright does not protect the idea, but only the expression of that idea.

A patent owner has the right to exclude others from "making, using, or selling" that which is covered by the patent.[1] As a result of a recent change in the law, the term of patents filed before 8 June 1995 is the longer of 17 years from the grant date or 20 years from the filing date. For patents filed after 8 June 1995, the term is 20 years from the filing date.[2] Extensions are available under limited circumstances.[3]

While the legal term of a patent is 20 years from the application's filing date, it would be naive to plan strategic decisions based on an expectation of 20 years of exclusivity in the marketplace. This is because the economic term of a patent is the shorter of this 20-year term and the life cycle of the technology covered by the patent. For different types of technology, the life cycle can differ widely. Using the pharmaceutical industry as an example, the technological life cycle of many beneficial drugs is much greater than 20 years — aspirin comes to mind. This is why a thriving generic industry exists in pharmaceuticals.

An example at the other end of the technological life cycle is, of course, the software industry. In the software industry, product and technological life cycles are often measured in months or years, not in decades. This economic term of a patent not only affects the value of patents, but given the time required to issue a patent — historically two to three years — the life cycle of some technologies may pass before the patent exists.

## Criteria for a Patent

To be entitled to a patent, two criteria must be satisfied. First, the invention must be patentable subject matter, which theoretically means it must relate to technology.[4] Second, the invention must represent a nonobvious advance over the existing state of the technology.[5] An alternative way to think of this latter requirement is that the invention must represent an "inventive step" over the existing state of the technology. If every element of an invention is described in a single "reference" (or source of prior art), the invention is said to lack "novelty." Even if every element is not found in a single reference, it may still be unpatentable. If the invention could have been readily deduced from the existing state of the technology by a hypothetical person with ordinary skill in the art, the invention is obvious and not entitled to a patent.[6]

Obviousness is based on consideration of four factors:

▸ The existing state of technology.

▸ The differences between the invention and the state of the "prior art." Prior art refers to the existing body of technological information against which a patent application is judged.

▸ The level of skill in the art. For example, the level of ordinary skill in the art could be an electrical engineer with at least a bachelor's degree with at least five years of experience in the applicable field.

▸ Objective evidence from the marketplace, if any.[7] Objective evidence from the actual marketplace setting in which an "invention" was made includes commercial success, long-felt need, unexpected results, failure of others, and favorable comments from objective sources.

In addition to advancing technology, to be patentable an invention must have "utility," that is, be useful.[8] Utility in this context is radically different from commercial viability. In most areas of technology, the utility standard is easy to meet. It is only necessary for some minimal level of usefulness to be present. For example, while utility for pure academic research is not enough,[9] utility for research on animals can be sufficient.[10]

## Patentable Subject Matter

The initial dividing line between patentable and unpatentable subject matter is the distinction between ideas and the useful application of ideas. Conceptual ideas are not patentable.[11] The law categorizes patentable subject matter as the more concrete "processes" or "products." The "products" category includes "machines, manufactures, and compositions of matter."[12]

Several examples refine the distinction between ideas and the useful application of ideas. A naturally occurring substance is not patentable, although a nonobvious refinement or application of a naturally occurring substance can be. A living substance can be patentable.[13] Printed matter is not patentable, although the physical structure of a product that includes printed matter can be, such as a train ticket. A mathematical formula is not patentable, although software can be.[14]

The more significant issue for patentable subject matter is the delay of the courts to accept emerging technologies as patentable subject matter. In the seventies, the courts struggled with biotechnology. (See Legal Focus: Patentability of Living Organisms, below.) More recently, courts have struggled with the patentability of software.

## Software

The historical development of the law alongside the technological development of the Internet frames the evolution of software as patentable subject matter. In recent years, the Internet has grown into an information superhighway consisting of an ever-expanding, interactive image and documentation system spanning an international network. While most users of the Internet believe it is a recent communications phenomenon, the origins of the Internet actually go back several decades.

Today's Internet grew out of a computer resource-sharing network created in the sixties by the government's Advanced Research Projects Agency. ARPA's chief scientist, Larry Roberts, was the primary designer of this network which was initially known as the ARPAnet. The initial problem facing Roberts was how to efficiently transmit digitized information in a reliable way. To solve this problem, in 1968 Roberts mandated use of packet switching in ARPA's Request for Proposals (RFP) to design the wide-area computer resource-sharing network.

Packet switching breaks up blocks of digitized information into smaller pieces called packets. These packets are transmitted through the network, usually by different routes, and are reassembled at their destination. Eight years before ARPA's RFP, Len Kleinrock invented packet switching.[15] Roberts believed Kleinrock's packet switching was the means to efficiently transmit digitized information in a reliable way. ARPA's RFP was awarded to a Cambridge, Massachusetts-based consulting group, Bolt, Beranek and Newman.

The next problem was how to interconnect a number of mainframe computers, most of which used different languages and different operating systems. Wesley Clark of Washington University in St. Louis devised the solution to this incompatibility problem. Clark proposed interfacing smaller minicomputers between every mainframe and the network. All of these minicomputers would run on the same operating system and use the same language. Each mainframe would only be required to interface with its dedicated minicomputer, with the minicomputer translating data from the mainframe into the network language and operating system.

It was left to a team from Bolt, Beranek and Newman, consisting of Bob Kahn, Severo Ornstein, and Dave Walden, to design these interface message processors (IMPs) — the predecessors to today's routers. With this basic design, the first two nodes on the ARPAnet communicated in October 1969.

All this development was done in the context of the existing paradigm that computer innovation was unpatentable subject matter. In 1972, the Supreme Court confirmed that pure software was not patentable subject matter by equating pure software to a mathematical algorithm, which was viewed as a "law of nature" and therefore unpatentable.[16] In 1978, the Supreme Court ruled software did not become patentable by the addition of "conventional, post-solution applications."[17] These decisions guided the reliance of the developing software industry on copyrights instead of patents.

By 1971, 15 nodes — mostly academic institutions — were up on the ARPAnet. However, the ARPAnet was not fulfilling its original goal. Resource sharing by the mainframe computers was simply too cumbersome. In March 1972, however, Ray Tomlinson of Bolt, Beranek and Newman invented e-mail. Use of this message transfer protocol quickly grew to be the major use of the ARPAnet.

By the middle of the seventies, several additional packet-switching networks existed alongside the ARPAnet. Once again, the compatibility problem emerged. Each of these different networks used a different protocol, making interconnection difficult. The solution — invented by Robert Kahn of ARPA and Vincent Cerf of Stanford University — was called the Transmission Control Protocol/Internet Protocol (TCP/IP). The Transmission Control Protocol packetized information and reassembled the information upon arrival. The Internet Protocol routed packets by encasing the packets between networks.[18] The ARPAnet adopted the Transmission Control Protocol/Internet Protocol in 1983. With the addition of the Domain Name System (DNS) in November 1983, the now familiar Internet address protocol was established.

Also in the seventies, a seemingly unrelated series of innovations occurred that would be essential to the development of the Internet. In the January 1975 issue of *Popular Electronics*, the Altair 8800 was introduced as the "world's first personal computer." The brainchild of Ed Roberts, the Altair 8800 was designed around an

Intel 8080 microprocessor that had been introduced in 1974. Soon the Altair 8800 was running on software written by Harvard University roommates Paul Allen and Bill Gates. The domain of personal computers was to remain largely in the realm of hobbyists for several years to come, with the first Apple computer introduced in 1976 and the IBM PC in 1981. Without the proliferation of personal computers, however, the ARPAnet likely would have remained an isolated academic phenomenon.

This development work still predated a shift in the paradigm away from software as unpatentable. In a series of decisions beginning in 1981, the Supreme Court and the Court of Appeals for the Federal Circuit (referred to as the Federal Circuit) increasingly accepted software as patentable subject matter. The Court of Appeals for the Federal Circuit is the Federal Appellate Court that has exclusive appellate jurisdiction over civil lawsuits that arise under the patent laws. In 1981, the Supreme Court ruled a process for curing rubber was patentable subject matter, even though all of the hardware involved in the curing process was well known, and the controlling software was the only new technology.[19] This decision formed the basis for the patent-drafting strategy of including hardware steps with software steps to achieve patentable subject matter.

In more recent cases, courts found patentable subject matter where the invention was increasingly pure software. In 1989, the Federal Circuit found that a voice-recognition software was patentable subject matter.[20] In 1992, the Federal Circuit found that software which used electro-cardiographic signals to determine a patient's susceptibility to heart attacks was patentable subject matter.[21] In 1994, the court found that logic which converted waveform data into pixel illumination data for display on an oscilloscope was patentable subject matter.[22]

These decisions gave rise to the patent-drafting strategy of framing an invention that includes software as a process directed to something other than software. For the examples above: a rubber-curing process instead of software for monitoring rubber curing; a voice-recognition apparatus instead of voice-recognition software; an electrocardiogram instead of software which analyzes an EKG signal; and a rasterizer instead of software which converts data.

These developments came too late for even the later innovations that created today's Internet. In 1990, Englishman Tim Berners-Lee of the European Center for Particle Research (CERN) in Switzerland invented the World Wide Web. This software, based on a program Berners-Lee wrote in 1980 to allow users to store information using random associations, allowed material from any computer, in any format, to be translated into a common language. Berners-Lee's invention established the three core components of the World Wide Web: the Universal Resource Locator (URL); HyperText Transfer Protocol (HTTP); and HyperText Markup Language (HTML). With the addition in 1991 of Java, a language that can be used to write programs for any platform and any application, developed by a team led by James Grosling at Sun Microsystems, the Internet as it is known today was established.

As the law exists today, software clearly qualifies as patentable subject matter in two "safe harbors": processes acting on physical subject matter, such as curing rubber in a mold; and processes involving real-world parameters, such as analyzing electrical signals representing human cardiac activity. If the invention is outside a safe harbor, it can still be patentable subject matter if it is a "practical application in the technical arts," such as a machine that produces a smooth waveform display.

In a much-publicized 1999 case, the paths of the Internet and the patent laws converged. The Federal Circuit ruled a financial service algorithm that moved electronic funds was patentable subject matter.[23] The higher court rejected the lower court's view that the subject matter was not patentable because it encompassed a business method. The publicity generated by this case has focused on the patentability of so-called "business-methods." While much of this publicity may well go too far — the court merely said the excuse that something was a business method was insufficient to preclude it as patentable subject matter — what this decision clarifies is that software innovations in the Internet are patentable subject matter. Although it has taken some time for the courts to catch up with the software industry, it is now an exceptional commercial software product for which the option of patent protection is unavailable.

## Inventive Step

Patentability is judged against the existing state of technology, but defining the state of technology can be challenging. Basically, the level of access to preexisting technology must be sufficient for the technology to fairly lie within the body of technological knowledge. Two types of triggering events place material in the existing state of technology. Material is included in the existing state of technology if it predates the date of invention.[24] This is referred to as an "anticipation." In addition, material is included in the existing state of technology if it was in existence more than twelve months before the date of application for a patent.[25] This is referred to as a "statutory bar."

The purposes of these two categories differ. Statutory bars target acts by the inventor. The twelve-month period is designed to allow the inventor some latitude in disclosing the invention before filing for a patent, although outside the United States such public disclosures can preclude patents (see International Considerations, below). On the other hand, most acts of anticipation would be impossible for the inventor; for example, how could an inventor disclose the invention before actual invention? This latitude is further expanded by the "experimental use" exception to the statutory bar. Under this exception, if the disclosure was necessary for experimental purposes, the twelve-month clock starts after the experimental use. An example of this would be road-paving technology, where the only way to test an innovation is to actually pave a road and let people drive on it. This is not considered public disclosure [26]

The most difficult determination of what is in the existing state of technology occurs when different inventors independently invent the same invention at about the same time. Unlike patent systems outside the United States, which are "first-to-file," the United States uses a so-called "first-to-invent" priority system. In this context, the inventive process is considered a three-step process.

"Conception" is the first step. Conception is the "formation in the inventor's mind of a definite perception of the complete and operative invention," that is, when the inventor unambiguously has a mental picture of the invention.[27] The last step is "reduction to practice." Reduction to practice arises when the product or process is produced or applied successfully. This can be no later than the time the patent application is filed, which becomes the date of reduction to practice if no actual reduction to practice occurred. The period between conception and reduction to practice must be bridged by due diligence in completing the invention. When two or more inventors apply for a patent on the same invention in the same time frame, an administrative lawsuit called an "interference" is held in the patent office to determine who first invented.[28]

## Inventorship

With the focus in the United States on individual rights, it is inventors who usually apply for patent applications. However, most inventors are under a separate legal obligation — such as an employment agreement — to assign their inventions to a corporation. An incorrect list of inventors can have serious consequences to a patent.

A patent application discloses an invention. An invention solves a problem. An inventor contributes to the solution of that problem. Conception requires both the idea of an inventive structure and possession of an operative method of making it. In this regard, conception requires more than a recognition of a desired result and more than a hope of a solution to a problem. Although for some technologies conception requires an actual working model — primarily in the biotechnology and chemical areas — conception typically occurs without an actual working model.

A patent application can name more than one inventor. When only one person solves a problem, sole invention occurs. When more than one person solves a problem, joint invention occurs. Joint invention also occurs when collaboration exists between two or more persons working toward the same solution. The collaboration may include mutual consultations and suggestions to develop the final concept, but the entire inventive concept need not occur to each of the inventors. The inventors need not physically work together on the project, but the collaboration required for joint invention is impossible when two persons are unaware of each other's work. It is not necessary that each inventor make the same amount of contribution. All that is required is each inventor make some contribution to the solution of the problem.

Although it is difficult to generalize about what contributions rise to the level of invention, certain acts are insufficient. The services, ideas, and aid of others is often used in the process of perfecting an invention. However, an inventor is not a person who:

- aids in perfecting the invention at the direction of another;
- follows the instructions of another in performing experiments;
- conducts analytical experiments to confirm another's work;
- suggests an idea of a result to be accomplished, rather than a means of accomplishing the result; and/or
- casually suggests some way to improve an invention, but takes no further role in incorporating the improvement.

However, a person who suggests an improvement to the invention is an inventor if the improvement rises to the level of invention itself.

From a practical standpoint, even if the list of inventors is wrong, judges hesitate to invalidate patents if the list was compiled in good faith. To ensure good faith, all of those involved in the project should be made aware a patent application is being prepared; this makes it difficult for someone who did not speak up at this time to later claim he or she should have been an inventor. If all those involved in the project agree to the list of inventors, the list is likely to be correct, and even if it is wrong, the list should be viewed as having been made in good faith. Avoid listing supervisors who did not participate in the project but insist on being included or dictate who should be listed. If those involved in the project disagree about who should be listed as inventors, the attorney assisting in the application should be consulted.

## Types of Patents

The three major types of patents are utility, design, and plant. A design patent excludes others from making, using, or selling designs that closely resemble a patented ornamental industrial design.[29] By definition, a design patent covers only the ornamental aspects and not the functionality of a product. A plant patent excludes others from replicating certain types of plants, for instance, asexually reproduced roses.[30]

The utility patent is the only form of intellectual property that can prevent duplication of the functional aspects of a product. Several different types of utility applications exist. The first type of utility application is a standard, newly filed original application. A continuation application is a second application filed while a first application is pending. The continuation application is for the same invention by the same inventor and contains the same description as the first application.[31] This application procedure is often used to make additional arguments to the patent office during the negotiation, or prosecution, of the application to secure a broader patent.

Another kind of application, made available by a recent change in the law, is a "provisional application." An inventor can use this procedure to file a technical disclosure of the invention in order to create a record at the patent office of the state of the invention as of the filing date. One drawback to a provisional application is that for a patent attorney to carefully craft a provisional patent disclosure, the cost of filing a provisional application may well approach the cost of filing a regular application. While submitting anything short of a well-thought-out application entails some risk, one strategy for inventors who cannot pay for a regular application is to draft a technical disclosure for a patent attorney to review and file as a provisional application. The patent attorney should take a couple of hours to review and revise the technical disclosure to minimize the risk that something in the disclosure, such as an admission of the state of the technology or the lack of alternative designs, will be used to limit the scope of the eventual patent.

Filing a provisional application buys the inventor about nine months before a standard patent application needs to be filed. For that part of the standard patent application which is described in the provisional application, the standard application is considered to have been filed on the filing date of the provisional application; however, any new information described in the standard application can only relate back to the filing date of the standard application. While filing a provisional allows inventors some latitude to disclose to third parties material which is described in the provisional application without compromising their rights, care should be taken not to disclose to third parties information developed after the provisional application is filed.

A continuation-in-part application is a second application filed after a standard application that adds additional information.[32] The continuation-in-part application is best viewed as a supplemental filing if further inventions related to the technology are made or if the commercial form of the technology evolves in an unexpected direction. The continuation-in-part application benefits from the earlier filing date of the first application for that part of the specification that is a part of the first application. That is, the part of the continuation-in-part that was included in the specification of the first application is considered, under law, to have the filing date of the first application. The new information disclosed in the continuation-in-part application can only benefit from the later continuation-in-part filing date.

A divisional application is a second application on a different invention that is carved out of a first application. Two or more independent and distinct inventions cannot be claimed in a single application.[33] A divisional application is typically filed when the patent office takes the position that an application covers more than one invention and issues a "restriction requirement," forcing the applicant to identify one invention per application.[34] Even though it is for a second invention, a divisional application discloses only the information contained in the first application.

Two types of applications apply to patents that have already issued. A reexamination application, which can be filed by anyone, reviews the correctness of the original issuance of the patent in view of newly discovered prior art.[35] A reissue application allows the patent owner to correct mistakes in the patent.[36] If the reissue application is filed within two years of when the original patent issued, the corrected mistake can be a broadening of the patent. This is typically done if the original patent is too narrow because the applicant failed to fully recognize the scope of the invention.

Those involved in the application process have ongoing duties that can affect the enforceability of the issued patent. Individuals involved in the process have a duty to disclose to the patent office all information of which they are aware that may be material to the patentability of the invention. An Information Disclosure Statement is the avenue by which this information is disclosed to the patent office. The duty to disclose continues throughout the application process; thus, Information Disclosure Statements should be filed whenever new information is discovered. Failure to disclose material information may render any issued patent unenforceable; willful failure can result in damages against the patent owner.

## Marking Patented Products

Products covered by a patent should be marked with a patent notice: "United States Patent No. [number]," or the abbreviated version, "U.S. Pat. No. [number]." If marking the product itself is difficult, the patent notice may be printed on a label applied to the product or related packaging. Proper labeling is important in assessing damages for an infringement. With a pending application, "Patent Applied For" can be used to give competitors notice of the possibility of the issuance of a patent in the future, although the application number should not be used.

## The Description of the Technology

The patent document itself includes a specification, claims, an abstract, and drawings, each of which has a specific purpose. The specification provides a description of the invention, and must satisfy "enablement" and "best mode" requirements.[37] To satisfy the enablement requirement, the description must be in such full, clear, and concise terms as to enable a person skilled in the art to make and use the invention. To satisfy the best mode requirement, the specification must contain a description of what the inventor believes to be the best form or embodiment of the invention at the time the application is filed. In other words, the inventor must completely describe the invention because, once a decision is made to file a patent application, the inventor cannot hold back information about the invention.

The abstract is a summary of the invention that allows a researcher to quickly obtain information about the invention. If an invention is capable of being drawn, drawings are used to facilitate an understanding of the invention.

As with patentable subject matter, enablement issues most often arise with emerging technologies. For example, early in the history of biotechnology, the issue of how to enable a person skilled in the art to replicate living matter caused much anxiety. This issue was ultimately resolved by requiring applicants for patents involving microorganisms or living cells to deposit a sample with a designated scientific institution so access could be provided to interested parties.[38]

Likewise, early in the history of software patents there were difficulties over the enablement requirement. Some attorneys believed source code had to be disclosed to satisfy the enablement requirement. Like manufacturing specifications of a mechanical device — which need not be disclosed — the better view is that source code need not be disclosed. This is good for patent applicants because, as with manufacturing specifications, inventors are understandably reluctant to expose their source code to competitors. Without disclosure of the source code, however, the enablement requirement must be satisfied by other descriptive means. In software and e-commerce patents, unique issues in drafting the application arise.

If an application for a mechanical or a hardware invention is drafted, much of the information required by the patent attorney is contained in the information developed to commercialize the product — often conveniently stored in a CAD (computer-assisted design) file. Likewise, in drafting an application for a chemical or biotechnology invention, laboratory notebooks typically include the experimental data used by the patent attorney. In software and e-commerce, however, the information needed to draft an application is often not produced in the commercialization of the product.

In drafting software and e-commerce applications, the best way to satisfy the enablement requirement is use of detailed flow charts to show and describe the logic flow of the software. Few software developers actually produce detailed flow charts as part of the software development process. Thus, unlike virtually every other technological field, to draft an application for software innovations someone must actually take the time to develop the information needed to describe the invention.

Obviously, the inventor is best equipped to do this. Unfortunately, much of the inventor's time and energy are focused on debugging the program to achieve a successful commercial product. Thus, the opportunity cost, that is, the cost of lost opportunities, of developing information to draft and file software patents can be significant.

## Mask Works

For the design of a semiconductor chip, the Semiconductor Chip Protection Act (SCPA) provides a type of protection that is a hybrid of patent and copyright.[39] The SCPA provides an exclusive right for ten years to reproduce the design of a semiconductor chip, known as a mask work; however, the SCPA includes several limitations that have restricted its usefulness.

To be entitled to protection, the SCPA draws from copyright the requirement of originality and the exclusion of the protection of ideas. Thus, the idea expressed in the mask work is not protected. The SCPA draws from patent the requirement of a level of novelty and nonobviousness. The SCPA specifically allows "reverse engineering" of a mask work and the use of the fruits of such reverse engineering in a new mask work, so long as the new mask work meets the originality requirement. A mask work must be registered within two years of disclosure or an offer to sell. Similar to the notice for copyrights, notice in the form of a circle surrounding an "M," the words "mask work," or the symbol "*M*" are not required, but give the owner procedural advantages.

## The Scope of the Patent

While the specification describes the invention, the claims define the scope of exclusivity reserved to the patent owner.[40] A claim sets the bounds of the technical area within which the patent owner has the right to exclude others from making, using, and selling the invention.[41] The claims of the patent define the exclusivity reserved to the patent owner in the same way as the metes and bounds of a real estate deed spell out the dimensions of a piece of property. Like a deed for land, each patent varies in scope, with narrow patents covering only the specific functional aspects of the invention while broad patents cover a broad range of functional equivalents. The breadth of the claims is not boundless; the invention as claimed must be the invention that is described in the specification.[42] The goal of patent drafting is to define the invention as broadly as legally permitted.

For a device to infringe a patent, the claim must describe or "read on" the device.[43] If each requirement of a claim reads on a device, the device is said to literally infringe the claim. If the equivalent of a requirement of a claim reads on a device, the device is said to infringe the claim under the "doctrine of equivalents." (See Doctrine of Equivalents, below.) If a requirement of the claim does not read on the device, infringement does not exist.[44]

By way of example, if a claim of a patent includes three requirements — a spring, a base, and a bar to retain the spring in a loaded state — a device that has those three elements infringes that claim. In order to avoid further nomenclature confusion, "requirements" refer to claim language, and "elements" to device (or process) structure. Devices that add additional elements — a device with a spring, a base, a bar to retain the spring in a loaded state, and a food platform — generally infringe. However, if a requirement is described narrowly as a species of the broader genus (a bar spring), the claim will not read on a device which has a different species of the same genus (a coiled spring). However, if the requirement is described broadly as the genus "spring," a device with either species — a bar spring or a coiled spring — infringes. Thus, less is often better: claims with fewer requirements and claims with broadly described requirements are more likely to be infringed.

## Types of Claims

Claims with fewer requirements and claims with broadly described requirements are more susceptible to an invalidity attack, usually accomplished by convincing a court that the claim was erroneously allowed by the patent office. In a very real sense, the more narrow the claim that is infringed, the less likely it will be invalidated. Thus, a well-drafted patent has claims of varying scope. One way to include claims of varying scope is to use both independent and dependent claims. An independent claim contains all of the claim requirements in one source. A dependent claim refers back to a previous claim, incorporates all of the requirements in the previous claim, and either adds or, more specifically, defines an existing requirement. The effect is that dependent claims define the invention more narrowly than independent claims. Thus, independent claims generally define the broadest scope of a patent, but dependent claims are more difficult to invalidate.

Another kind of claim, a method claim, defines the invention by a series of steps to be followed in performing a process. This type of claim is contrasted with an apparatus claim, which defines the invention structurally. A Jepson claim is a specialized type of claim that uses a format in which the old elements of the invention are first set forth, followed by the new requirements of the invention.[45]

## Doctrine of Equivalents

The difficulty of describing an inventive concept in words is recognized in a rule referred to as the "doctrine of equivalents." Under this doctrine, even if the actual language of the claim does not literally read on a device, if the "accused product or process contain[s] elements ... equivalent to each claimed [requirement] of the patented invention," the device may still infringe.[46] To infringe under the doctrine of equivalents, each requirement or its equivalent must be present in the accused device.[47]

This doctrine focuses on two inquiries: for chemical cases, the focus is the interchangeability of the elements; for mechanical cases, the focus is whether the element performs substantially the same function in substantially the same way to accomplish the same result as the patented requirement.[48] For electrical and software cases, either inquiry can apply.

However, comments made by the patent applicant to the patent office in arguing for the grant of the patent can narrow the scope of equivalents under the doctrine.[49] Just as the intent of the parties to a contract can be clarified by reviewing the contract negotiation, the intended scope of a claim requirement can be clarified by reviewing the negotiation of the patent with the patent office. Thus, not all requirements of a claim are equal. If, in securing the patent, the applicant focused on the importance of a specific requirement, the language of that requirement will be interpreted more narrowly than a requirement not so emphasized. These negotiations are referred to as a "patent prosecution" and are memorialized in correspondence between the patent applicant and the patent office, known as a "prosecution history."

A corollary to the doctrine of equivalents is the "reverse doctrine of equivalents." Under this doctrine, even if the claims seem to literally read on the device under investigation, if the device is so far changed that it performs the function in a substantially different way, the device will not infringe.[50]

## The Exclusionary Right

One of the most confusing concepts in the laws of patents is the relationship or, more accurately, the lack of a relationship between patentability and infringement. Many managers believe that when a patent issues, the patent carries an affirmative right to commercialize that technology. This is not the case. A patent gives the patent owner the right to exclude others from making, using, or selling what is within the scope of the patent. The patent does not give the patent owner the affirmative right to commercialize the invention. "A patent is not the grant of a right to make or use or sell. It does not, directly or indirectly, imply any such right. It grants only the right to exclude others."[51] Thus, patentability is a separate issue from infringement.

As with many areas of patent law, an analogy can be drawn to real property — although the analogy cannot be stretched very far. The ownership of real property does not necessarily give owners the right to any use of their property. For example, zoning laws restrict the use of property to certain types of structures, while environmental laws restrict use of property as dumping grounds for hazardous wastes. Likewise, the patent grant gives the patent owner no affirmative right to commercialize the technology if it infringes other third party rights.

A patent can be issued for an invention when that invention is sufficiently distinct from the prior art. In this inquiry, the scope of the claims of any prior art patents is not considered when deciding whether the invention represents an inventive step. If the scope of preexisting patents from a prior invention encompasses the commercial embodiment of the invention, the owner of the prior patent can preclude the owner of the later patent from commercializing the improved technology. Likewise, the owner of the later patent can preclude the owner of the prior patent from commercializing the prior invention in the form of the improvement that is encompassed by the later patent, even though this also is encompassed by the prior patent. When this occurs, the patents are said to "mutually block" each other. "[T]hat someone has a patent right to exclude others from making the invention claimed in his patent does not mean that his invention cannot infringe claims of another patent broad enough to encompass, i.e. to 'dominate' his invention."[52] (See Chapter 6: Patent Charting.)

In fact, most patents are improvements over prior technology. If a patent on the prior technology exists, it is likely that the improved version of the technology will be encompassed within the scope of that prior patent. This does not always create a problem — the same company often issues patents on base technology as well as improvements to that technology. While these patents are mutually blocking, no conflict arises because the same entity owns both. A conflict arises when two different entities own the two blocking patents. When this conflict occurs, it is only by a cross-license that the improved version of the technology can be commercialized. (See Legal Focus: Mutually Blocking Patents, below.)

## The Patent Challenged – Invalidity

Once issued, a patent is by law presumed valid.[53] While a challenger to a patent carries a fairly high burden in invalidating the patent, this burden is more easily overcome when relevant prior art is uncovered that was not considered by the patent examiner when originally issuing the patent.[54] Typically, patent office records are searched for this state-of-the-art determination. In some fields, however, much of the evidence of the state of the art is not found in patent office records. Because of the historical development of software patents, the issue of nonobviousness for software and e-commerce patents involves problems unique to this technological area. While all issued patents are presumed valid, it is particularly difficult to determine the state of the art in software fields. Because for many years software was not thought to be patentable, most of the evidence of the state of the art in software is not found in the patent office records.

This can be contrasted with other technological fields such as pharmaceuticals where, because patents have long been the primary source of protection for new developments, the patent office records are an extremely good indicator of the state of the art. It is expensive to search beyond the patent office records to determine the state of the art. Because patent office examiners typically do not have the resources to search outside the patent office, as a practical matter many practitioners view the presumption of validity for software and e-commerce patents to be weaker than for other patents. This means that even if a patent is issued on a software or e-commerce innovation, competitors may only reluctantly respect those rights, forcing the patent owner into expensive and risky litigation. From this perspective, the value of software and e-commerce patents suffers.

In determining the existing state of technology against which an invention is judged, prior art can include patents, books, journal articles, abstracts, advertisements, promotional literature, and other publications. Prior art also can include public disclosure or commercial activity occurring more than one year before the filing date of the application. This can be an actual sale or conversations that might be viewed as offers for sale, exhibits at a trade show, or other public display. In order for sales activity to bar a patent, the invention must be developed sufficiently so an application could have been filed, and the sales activity must be primarily for profit rather than for experimental purposes.[55]

To gain some insight into obviousness, economic evidence, specifically from the real-world marketplace, is considered. Such evidence is referred to as the "objective criteria" of patentability. Evidence from which it logically follows that the invention was not obvious fits into this category. Examples include:

- ▶ Commercial success — when the market enthusiastically receives a new product, it logically follows the new product is inventive.
- ▶ Long-felt but unfulfilled need — if in a particular technological field recognition of a need exists and a new product fills that need, it logically follows the new product is inventive.
- ▶ Unexpected results — if the results of an experiment are surprising, it logically follows the results are inventive.
- ▶ Failure of others — when others have tried and failed to solve the technological problem solved by an invention, it logically follows the solution is inventive.
- ▶ Industry acquiescence — when others in the industry have licensed the patent, it logically follows the patent is valid.
- ▶ Favorable comments from objective sources — when commentators such as the trade press or even an accused infringer laud a new product, it logically follows the new product is inventive.

## International Considerations

Despite focus on differences between U.S. patents and patent systems outside the United States, the patent systems in Western Europe and Japan are remarkably similar to the U.S. system. U.S. patent law grew out of English patent law, which is part of European patent law. Japanese patent law was originally modeled on German patent law. The net effect is a similarity in most provisions of the patent laws in the United States, Western Europe, and Japan.

If anything, these similarities have tended to lull managers into complacency in managing foreign patents. Thus, an entrepreneurial manager should understand the differences.

One difference is most countries require "absolute novelty." In the United States, a patent applicant has a 12-month "grace period" after a public disclosure or commercial sales activity in which to file for patent protection. In countries outside the United States, the absolute novelty requirement — precluding many forms of disclosure of the invention and many types of commercial activity before the effective filing date of a patent application — could bar issuance of a patent. These patent systems outside the United States are referred to as "absolute novelty systems."

The absoluteness of absolute-novelty countries is tempered by international treaties establishing procedural reciprocity with regard to the physical act of filing the application. Pursuant to these treaties, applications filed outside the United States within twelve months of the U.S. filing date are considered under the law to have been filed on the earlier U.S. filing date. Thus, if the invention is disclosed or commercial activity undertaken after a U.S. filing date, the treaty avoids the absolute-novelty bar that might otherwise preclude a foreign patent.

Given this absolute novelty requirement, waiting for marketplace feedback will almost certainly be fatal to patent protection outside the United States. Even with the grace period in the United States, marketplace feedback often is not received within a year, even on eventually successful products. Thus, entrepreneurial managers philosophically view patent expenses as part of the up-front research and development investment that is necessary to develop new products. Entrepreneurial managers accept that these expenses are incurred before customers pass judgment on the new products.

Another difference between the patent system of the United States and those of other countries, the confidentiality of pending applications, has been mitigated in concessions made in trade negotiations. Until recently, applications filed in the United States were kept confidential until the application matured into an issued patent. Thus, there was no way of finding out what was in the pipeline at the U.S. Patent Office. This was in contrast to countries outside the United States, where applications are published — "laid open," in patent parlance — 18 months after filing. As a result of a recent change in the law, U.S. applications now will be published 18 months after filing; however, if the applicant is willing to forego patent filings in countries outside the United States, publication can be stopped and the application will remain confidential.

A third difference is when the patent can be challenged. In the United States, a third party cannot formally challenge the issuance of a patent, but must wait until after the patent has issued. In contrast, outside the United States the acceptance of a patent can be challenged before issuance in a procedure referred to as an "opposition." An opposition is an administrative lawsuit in which evidence and arguments are presented to persuade a patent office not to issue the patent. Outside the United States, oppositions can be an important strategy in avoiding conflicts with competitors' patents.

1st
Difference

2nd
Difference

3rd
Difference

Finally, many countries outside the United States provide an additional category of patent protection, which, while known by many different names, is often called a "utility model." This form of protection neither requires the same degree of inventive step nor extends the same scope of protection as regular patents. It effectively bars direct copying, but not independent development of a product. Nevertheless, because of the absence of such protection in the United States, U.S. companies often fail to utilize these utility model patents to protect such so-called minor innovations outside the United States. An entrepreneurial manager recognizes the opportunity to file utility model applications in countries where a market for such products exists, in order to protect minor innovations outside the United States.

## Where to File

Provided the absolute novelty conditions are satisfied, where to file applications outside the United States is a business decision. Typical factors considered by entrepreneurial managers include:

- ► commercial potential,
- ► importance of the invention,
- ► economic significance of the market,
- ► likely location of a competitive manufacturing facility,
- ► likelihood that a competitor would compete in the market,
- ► strength of available protection, and
- ► costs of filing.

These decisions are best made on a strategic geographic basis. For example, if protection in South America is desired for a cattle-breeding technology, several South American countries — such as Argentina, Brazil, and Colombia — can be strategically chosen. Likewise, if protection in northern Europe is desired for a cold weather automotive technology, several northern European countries — such as Holland, Germany, and Sweden — can be selected. By strategically choosing countries across a geographic region, entrepreneurial managers can create an economic disincentive for competition by eliminating economies of scale across the region without incurring the costs of patenting the invention in every country.

There are basically two ways to file applications outside the United States. Applications can be filed directly in the patent offices of individual countries or regions across the world. Alternatively, a single application can be filed with the World Intellectual Property Organization (WIPO) under the International Patent Corporation Treaty (PCT). This PCT application is best viewed as buying an option to file national or regional applications in designated countries or regions.

Filing through the PCT does not eliminate the costs or requirements of filing directly in the national or regional patent offices, but defers the expenditures for 20 to 30 months after the U.S. filing date. Filing under the PCT is cost-effective when a significant number of countries — such as more than four — are considered for national or regional filing. Filing through the PCT is typically done if the applicant believes additional information about the invention will become available before the deadline to exercise the option. If this additional information leads to the decision to abandon the applications, the costs of national or regional filings are avoided. When filing through the PCT, entrepreneurial managers typically list broadly the countries in which they wish to maintain an option, because if a country is not listed it cannot be added later.

A major regional patent system is the European Patent Organization (EPO). The EPO member countries are Austria, Belgium, Cyprus, Denmark, Finland, France, Germany, Greece, Ireland, Italy, Liechtenstein, Luxembourg, Monaco, the Netherlands, Portugal, Spain, Sweden, Switzerland, Turkey, and the United Kingdom. The EPO is like the PCT in that, to have effect, a fee must be paid to register the European patent in member countries. However, the EPO is different from the PCT in that the EPO offers a more substantive examination of the application. It is because of this difference, and the avoidance of the expense of separate substantive examinations in each country, that entrepreneurial managers choose the European regional patent if protection is desired in three or more EPO member countries.

## The "Intellectual Property" Company

CASE
STUDY

Perhaps no company in the history of American business has had a stronger reliance on intellectual property than Xerox. As late as 1957, the state of copying technology was not impressive. Mimeography involved typing a document on a special carbon paper, carefully placing the carbon in a machine, and "running off" copies, often by hand-cranking the machine. However, the 20-year obsession of a young patent attorney in Rochester, New York, changed the industry.

In 1935, 29-year-old Chester Carlson, who, like all patent attorneys, studied technology as an undergraduate (physics at the California Institute of Technology) before entering the law, learned of the work of a Hungarian scientist who used powder and static electricity to replicate photographs. With the help of Otto Kornei, a German-born physicist, Carlson spent the next three years experimenting with different chemicals and methods, trying to develop an efficient paper-copying process. In October 1938, he successfully tested a complex, five-step process that used electric charges, powder, and heat to create images. As a patent attorney, Carlson took an aggressive patent strategy, filing several applications on these innovations.

Recognizing that he needed a corporate partner to commercialize his new technology, Carlson approached companies like IBM, Kodak, and Radio Corporation of America. Twenty companies refused him before he found a taker. Dr. R.M. Schaffert was head of the Graphics Arts Division at Battelle Memorial Institute, a nonprofit research institute in Columbus, Ohio. In 1944 the Battelle Memorial Institute secured a 60 percent interest in Carlson's work and together they further developed the technology. The Battelle Memorial Institute also continued Carlson's patent strategy, aggressively filing patent applications on the innovations they developed.

Also in 1944, the head of Haloid Corporation in Rochester, New York, faced a problem. The grandson of a founder, Joseph Wilson saw the market for his company's photographic paper and supplies dwindling as World War II drew to a close. Haloid desperately needed to expand into a new market to keep its public investors happy.

Haloid's head of Research and Development saw an article in Kodak's *Monthly Abstract Bulletin* about Carlson's work at the Battelle Memorial Institute. Because the process used a treated paper, the potential fit with Haloid's business was clear. They negotiated a license to the technology for a $25,000 yearly payment and an eight-percent royalty on future sales.

The first step towards commercialization for Haloid was to name the process. In 1948, a Battelle researcher and an Ohio State University professor of classics coined a new term "xerography," from the Greek meaning "dry writing." As a coined term with no descriptive connection to Carlson's process, the term "xerography" was entitled to a broad scope of trademark protection. The term xerography would give rise to the brand name Xerox, which was to become one of the strongest and best-recognized trademarks in the world. At an October 1948 press conference at the Optical Society of America conference in Detroit, Michigan, the process was uncovered. Joseph Wilson's father, himself a former head of Haloid, predicted, "The first commercial adaptation of xerography, the Xerox Copier Machine, Model A, will be made in 1950."

Unfortunately, this brash prediction proved wishful thinking — the first Xerox copier was not introduced until 1959. As Haloid struggled towards commercialization, it sustained itself with a succession of products based in part on the xerography process. For example, in 1955 it introduced an automated machine that could make prints from microfilm. In 1956 it bought the four basic xerography patents from Battelle Memorial Institute. With these and its own patents from its continuation of Carlson's aggressive patent strategy, it was able to keep much-better-funded companies like Kodak, 3M, and Smith-Corona from utilizing xerography in their copier research. By 1966 Xerox had issued 500 patents on xerography.

In anticipation of the introduction of the Xerox copier, in the mid-fifties the company changed its name to Haloid-Xerox, Inc. In 1956 it entered into a partnership named Rank-Xerox with a British conglomerate to sell outside the United States. When the product was ready — dubbed the 914 because it could copy paper up to nine by fourteen inches — it had a sticker price of $29,500. Realizing this amount would limit its market, Haloid-Xerox devised an alternative pricing strategy.

The units were leased for $95 a month, which included 2,000 free copies, with customers paying four cents for each copy over 2,000.

The product was an immediate success. Between 1959 and 1961, Haloid-Xerox's revenues nearly doubled. By 1962, following another name change — this time to Xerox Corporation — sales were $176 million. By 1969, Xerox had a market capitalization of $8.2 billion. All this resulted from an obsessive idea of a 29-year-old patent attorney and an aggressive intellectual property strategy.

CASE
STUDY

CONT.

## Mutually Blocking Patents

Legal Focus

A patent gives the patent owner the right to exclude others from making, using, or selling what is within the scope of the patent for a period of 20 years from application. The patent does not give the patent owner the affirmative right to commercialize the invention. These difficult concepts can be better understood with an historical example.

The most famous instance of mutually blocking patents occurred at the infancy of the radio industry. In 1905, U.S. Patent No. 803,684, titled "Instrument for Converting Alternating Electric Currents into Continuous Currents," was issued to Sir John Ambrose Fleming of Great Britain. This patent described the vacuum tube diode. The diode allows current to flow in one direction but blocks current flow in the reverse direction. This feature can be used to rectify alternating current. The Fleming vacuum diode represented a significant technological improvement and therefore was awarded a broad patent.

Shortly after Fleming's invention, Dr. Lee DeForest developed the vacuum tube triode. This device was issued three U.S. patents: U.S. Patent No. 824,637 issued 26 June 1906; U.S. Patent No. 836,070 issued 13 November 1906; and U.S. Patent No. 879,532 issued 18 February 1908. The DeForest vacuum tube triode allowed use of much weaker signals, which allowed for much greater distance reception. DeForest's vacuum tube triode was a huge commercial success, forming the basis for receiving all transmitted signals, including high fidelity radio and television, up to and beyond the invention of the transistor in 1947.

DeForest was awarded a patent on his vacuum tube triode because it involved an inventive step over the Fleming device. However, Fleming's earlier patent was broad enough to cover DeForest's vacuum tube triode. Thus, the vacuum tube triode infringed Fleming's vacuum tube diode patent. However, even though the vacuum tube triode offered significant commercial advantages over the vacuum tube diode, DeForest's patents prevented Fleming's use of the vacuum tube triode.[56]

Without some form of cross-license, both inventors were precluded from making, using, or selling the vacuum tube triode. Of course, no one else could make, use, or sell the vacuum tube triode in the United States.

This stalemate helped lead to the creation of the Radio Corporation of America in 1919. While superior radios were available outside the United States, only radios of inferior capability were available in the United States as a result of the patent situation. At the prompting of Franklin D. Roosevelt, then Under Secretary of the Navy, the General Electric Corporation formed the Radio Corporation of America, in part to acquire the Fleming and DeForest patents.

**Legal Focus**

## Patentability of Living Organisms

Like computer innovation, the development of biotechnology as an emerging industry bore the burden of the courts' struggle with the patentability of emerging technologies. Similar to the equating of pure software to a mathematical algorithm, the challenge in finding biotechnology innovations patentable was to overcome the prohibition against patenting "products of nature."

In 1948, for example, the Supreme Court ruled that a mixed culture of *Rhizobium* bacteria capable of inoculating several groups of plants could not be patented. The *Rhizobium* bacteria enabled certain plants to draw nitrogen from the air and transform it to a solid. Difference species of the *Rhizobium* bacteria were effective for different types of plants. The inventor discovered that certain strains of inoculates of the bacteria genus *Rhizobium* were mutually noninhibitive with certain strains of other species. He thus produced a mixed culture of *Rhizobium* bacteria capable of inoculating several groups of plants. The Supreme Court found the patent invalid because the bacteria were considered a "work of nature."[57]

Against this backdrop, in 1977 the Supreme Court again took on the issue.[58] A microbiologist employed by General Electric, Ananda Chakrabarty used genetic engineering to create a new strain of bacteria from the genus *Pseudomonas*. This new strain of bacteria had an improved capacity to degrade crude oil. This had significant commercial potential for cleaning oil spills. The U.S. Patent Office rejected General Electric's attempt to patent his invention. General Electric appealed to the Supreme Court.

The issue before was whether a living organism could be patented. The Supreme Court decided it could. The Supreme Court distinguished this case from the "laws of nature" cases, because Chakrabarty's new strain of *Pseudomonas* bacteria was "markedly different . . . from any found in nature."[59]

Despite this, the patent office apparently was not convinced that all living organisms were patentable. In 1984, Standish Allen, Jonathan Chaiton, and Sandra Downing filed an application for a method for producing sterile Pacific oysters. Naturally occurring oysters are not edible when they are breeding in the summer months — hence the axiom that oysters are edible during months that include the letter "r." The advantage to sterile oysters is they do not reproduce, making them edible all year around.[60]

The patent examiner denied the patent on the grounds the claimed product was a living entity. While the patent was ultimately rejected as obvious over the existing state of oyster-breeding technology, the appeals board within the patent office determined this living entity was patentable subject matter. This case appears to finally have convinced the patent office that living organisms are patentable. In 1988, the patent office issued U.S. Patent No. 4,736,866, directed at a rodent genetically engineered to grow cancer cells — affectionately known as the "Harvard mouse."

## The Federal Circuit                                             Legal Focus

The current strength in the economic value of patents resulted from what M.B.A.s term an "environmental change." In 1982, Congress created a centralized, specialized appeals court for virtually all patent cases, regardless of where they originate. The Federal Circuit was created in 1982 by the merger of two existing courts: the Court of Claims and the Court of Customs and Patent Appeals.[61] Prior to 1982, twelve regional circuit courts of appeals heard appeals from patent cases from federal district courts in their regions. For example, the Second Circuit heard appeals from the Southern District of New York, the Seventh Circuit heard appeals from the Northern District of Illinois, and the Ninth Circuit in California heard appeals from the Central District of California. The Court of Customs and Patent Appeals heard appeals from the patent office while the Court of Claims heard claims for patent infringement against the United States.

The Federal Courts Improvement Act of 1982 withdrew jurisdiction for patent appeals from the twelve regional courts of appeals and vested almost exclusive patent appellate jurisdiction in the newly created Federal Circuit. The legislative history notes three reasons for creating this specialized court: first, to reduce the workload of the regional courts of appeals;[62] second, to make more effective use of judicial resources by eliminating overlap between the Court of Claims and the Court of Customs and Patent Appeals.[63]

The third and most compelling reason for the creation of the Federal Circuit was to obtain greater uniformity in patent law, thereby making patents more stable and predictable.[64] Prior to the centralization of appellate patent authority, there was great divergence in the interpretation of the patent laws among the regional courts of appeals. This divergence lead to uncertainty in the application of the law, "forum shopping," and a general degradation of the value of patents.

After its creation, the Federal Circuit addressed this third reason with a vengeance. Before its creation, about 70 percent of patents that were litigated were found either invalid or not infringed — the patent owner lost. After its creation, the statistics reversed; now, nearly 70 percent of litigated patents are found to be infringed. Apparently comfortable with this development, the Supreme Court took a decidedly nonactivist attitude towards patents for nearly 15 years after the creation of the Federal Circuit. During this period the Supreme Court decided only two patent appeals from the Federal Circuit.[65] This contrasts with the recent willingness of the Supreme Court to decide patent issues. In five cases over the last four years, the Supreme Court decided patent cases. In some of these cases, the legal issues were unremarkable. However, that the Supreme Court accepted and decided these issues may signal a developing mistrust of the Federal Circuit by the Supreme Court.

An example is the 1999 decision in *Dickinson v. Zurko*, which involved the standard of review of patent office decisions.[66] In a 6–3 decision, the Supreme Court overturned the unanimous Federal Circuit and ruled the Federal Circuit must give more deference to the patent office in reviewing its decisions. The actual legal issue was not very significant — even the Court's decision admitted as much. The three justices that disagreed with the decision made the point they would defer to the specialized Federal Circuit on these issues. This inferentially means the other six justices see no reason to defer to the Federal Circuit on patent issues.

Also telling is the Supreme Court's 1998 interpretation of the so-called "on-sale" bar.[67] The on-sale bar prohibits a patent on an invention that has been on sale more than one year before filing the application. In *Pfaff v. Wells Electronics, Inc.*, the issue was whether this one-year bar applies even if the invention has not been completed — in the language of the patent laws, "reduced-to-practice."[68]

The Federal District Court in Fort Wayne, Indiana found Pfaff's patent valid and infringed by Wells Electronics. Despite the patent owner's efforts to "sell" more than one year before the application was filed, the District Court rejected the invalidity defense because the application was filed less than one year after the invention was reduced-to-practice.[69]

A unanimous panel of the Federal Circuit reversed.[70] As long as the invention was "substantially complete at the time of sale," the one-year clock ran even though the invention was not reduced-to-practice.[71] The Federal Circuit applied a "totality of the circumstances" test under which "all of the circumstances surrounding the sale or offer to sell, including the stage of development of the invention and the nature of the invention, must be considered and weighed."[72]

The Supreme Court rejected this "totality of the circumstances" test. Instead, the Supreme Court applied a two-part test: "First, the product must be the subject of a commercial offer for sale."[73] "Second, the invention must be ready for patenting."[74] Thus, the Supreme Court reviewed a case about a relatively narrow legal patent issue to which the Federal Circuit applied a consistent standard. Amazingly, the Supreme Court justified its review of the case in view of conflicting decisions of two regional appeals courts, citing 20-year-old decisions from the Seventh and Second Circuits.[75]

This reference to these 20-year-old decisions, of course, makes little sense in view of the centralized authority in patent appeals since the creation of the Federal Circuit in 1982. The centralization of the patent laws eliminated one of the most persuasive arguments for the Supreme Court to accept patent cases: conflicts among the regional courts of appeals. Indeed, in 1993 the Supreme Court itself noted, "[a]s a matter of practice, the possibility that we would ... review [the Federal Circuit's] resolution of an infringement issue is extremely remote ...."[76]

While *Wells Electronics* offers telling evidence of the Supreme Court's willingness to review decisions of the Federal Circuit, two preceding decisions provide further evidence of the developing rift between the Federal Circuit and the Supreme Court. Just one and a half years before issuing its decision in *Wells Electronics*, in 1997 the Supreme Court issued its landmark decision about the doctrine of equivalents.[77] The logic in reviewing this case was more typical — the appeal was from a deeply divided decision of the Federal Circuit.

However, the ultimate ruling suggested something had changed in the relationship between the Federal Circuit and the Supreme Court. Indeed, the Supreme Court found the dissenting opinion of the late Judge Nies persuasive, thus leaving the Supreme Court concurring with a Federal Circuit judge no longer on the bench.[78]

During the prosecution of the patent the applicant entered a narrowing claim amendment, which was apparently not required to distinguish over the prior art. In amending the claims, the applicant distinguished the invention over the prior art at one end of a defined range. The limitation that was added at the other end of the range lacked any corresponding explanation. The issue in the case was whether this claim amendment could be expanded under the doctrine of equivalents. The Federal Circuit was divided into two schools of thought. One school strongly supported the application of the doctrine of equivalents.[79] The opposing school argued that the doctrine should be eliminated as an improper expansion of the scope of the claims.[80] Judge Nies took a middle ground, arguing that the doctrine should apply but be limited to an element-by-element analysis.[81]

The Supreme Court rejected the argument that a claim cannot be expanded regardless of the reason for the amendment. Rather, the Supreme Court held the reason for the amendment must be examined, with only amendments made to avoid prior art limiting the expansion of the claim under the doctrine of equivalents.

In clarifying the doctrine, the Supreme Court ruled the "doctrine of equivalents must be applied to individual [requirements] of the claim, not to the invention [or claim] as a whole."[82] The Supreme Court also ruled evidence of intent — either of copying as evidence of infringement or of design around as evidence of noninfringement — "plays no role in the application of the doctrine of equivalents."[83] To "design around" is to design a product to compete with, but not infringe upon, a patented product.

The Supreme Court further decided that under the doctrine, equivalents are not limited to those disclosed in the patent itself or even to those known at the time the patent was issued, but can extend to later technology. Finally, the Supreme Court gave considerable support to the view that the doctrine is for a jury to decide, although the Supreme Court specifically disclaimed deciding this issue. Thus, while striking the middle ground, the Supreme Court gave an endorsement to the doctrine of equivalents. Significantly, the Supreme Court was at odds with both the Federal Circuit majority that wanted an even broader expansion of the doctrine and the dissent that wanted to do away with the doctrine entirely.[84]

In 1996, just one year before deciding *Hilton Davis*, the Supreme Court — again unanimously — decided *Markman v. Westview Instruments*.[85] This case determined the interpretation of the claims in a patent is the role of the judge and not the jury. At trial, the jury found an infringement of the patent after hearing testimony from a witness about the meaning of the claims.[86] After trial, the judge overturned the jury based on his interpretation of the claims. The Federal Circuit affirmed, ruling the interpretation of the claims to be the role of the judge.[87]

After a lengthy review of the historical arguments on the interpretation of claims, a unanimous Supreme Court affirmed the Federal Circuit. Interestingly, not once did the Supreme Court discuss the view of the specialized patent court in explaining its affirmation. Significantly, the Supreme Court again reviewed a Federal Circuit decision in which little controversy existed; the Federal Circuit's opinion was joined by eight of its eleven judges.

This lack of trust of the Federal Circuit by the Supreme Court could have significant implications not only for developing case law but also for issues thought to be settled. The Supreme Court appears to support strong patents but is uncomfortable with the degree of ambiguity in interpreting patents left by past Federal Circuit decisions. Indeed, until the Supreme Court gives its view, the law may well remain unsettled on issues such as:

- ▸ Fallout from the *Hilton Davis* decision.
- ▸ The patentability of business methods.[88]
- ▸ The scope of functional claim language.[89]
- ▸ The applicability of the doctrine of equivalents.[90]
- ▸ The standard for actual controversy for a declaratory judgment.[91]
- ▸ The standard for antitrust liability in patent cases.[92]

## The Debate About Functional Language

Among the unsettled issues remaining in the patent laws is the proper interpretation of claims that include "functional" language. Some poorly chosen language in several Federal Circuit cases, which appears to have significantly narrowed the scope of functional language, has caused many patent attorneys to avoid the use of functional language altogether, believing structural language is broader. This possible error should be of little consequence because, under proper claim-drafting practice, claims with both structural and functional language can and should be employed. More

Legal Focus
continued

dangerously, in advising clients about the scope of competitive patents, many patent attorneys may be too narrowly interpreting functional language by reading specific structure from the specification as further requirements of the functional language. Until this issue is settled, entrepreneurial managers would be wise to exercise caution in narrowly interpreting functional language.

The debate about functional language stems from the dual role of the patent. The first role of the patent is to sufficiently describe the invention. The second role of the patent is to define the exclusionary grant to the patent owner. The claims of a patent are the vehicle used to define this exclusionary grant.[93] Claims map out the scope of exclusivity in the same way the legal description of land maps out the metes and bounds of a real estate deed. Thus, claims with broadly described requirements are more likely to be infringed.

One attempt to broaden a claim is to describe function instead of structure. In a simple example, the spring of a mousetrap might be described as a "means for biasing" rather than as a "spring." The drafter's hope is this language not only reads on a spring but also on equivalent structures, such as an elastic band. From a societal standpoint, however, too broad a reading of such functional language not only encompasses technologies that provide appropriate economic incentive to encourage innovation but also different structures that could unduly restrict competition.

The use of functional language in claims is not new. In the *Telegraph* case of 1854, the Supreme Court decided that one of Samuel Morse's claims for the means of using electro-magnetism to communicate at a distance was invalid.[94] Thus, the Supreme Court rejected a claim in which the invention was entirely defined in functional language. Later Supreme Court cases also followed this view.[95]

The Supreme Court's 1881 decision in *Continental Paper Bag v. Eastern Paper Bag* appeared to contradict the *Telegraph* case.[96] The Supreme Court decided claims that included functional language were infringed by a later-developed, alternative structure for achieving the same function. This implicit approval resulted in widespread use of functional language in the early 1900s. The apparent conflict with the *Telegraph* case was dismissed because the *Telegraph* case dealt with a claim with only one requirement, while the later case dealt with a claim with more than one requirement including a functional requirement.

However, in 1946 the implicit approval of functional language was explicitly rejected by the Supreme Court in *Halliburton v. Walker*.[97] The regional Circuit Court of Appeals for the Ninth Circuit ruled a claim with functional language infringed. The Ninth Circuit distinguished the *Telegraph* case as involving a single means claim (one requirement) while the patent at issue was a combination invention (more than one requirement) which included a functional requirement.[98]

The Supreme Court rejected this distinction; it considered all functional language too broad. The Supreme Court felt an accurate definition of the scope of the invention should be confined to the specific structure described in the patent. This decision led to Congress' review of the issue of functional language in patent claims.

In 1952, Congress sanctioned use of functional language and effectively overruled the *Halliburton* case by adding a paragraph to the law:

> [A requirement] in a claim for a combination may be expressed as a means or step for performing a specified function without the recital of structure, material, or acts in support thereof, and such a claim shall be construed to cover the corresponding structure, material, or acts described in the specification and equivalents thereof.[99]

While approving functional language, Congress defined the boundaries on the use of functional language. The functional language must utilize a specific format: either "means-plus-function" — like "means for biasing" — or "step-plus-function." The claim must include more than one requirement; a claim with a single requirement cannot be functional.[100] The functional language must be adequately supported in the detailed description.[101] Claims that employ functional language also must be sufficiently clear to "particularly point out and distinctly claim" the invention.[102]

In 1992, the view of the Federal Circuit was added to the fray.[103] Early Federal Circuit decisions often contained careless statements that were interpreted as expanding the scope of functional language. In 1985 in *D.M.I. v. Deere & Co.*, for example, the Federal Circuit stated that:

> ... patentees are required to disclose in the specification some enabling means for accomplishing the function set forth in the "means plus function" [requirement]. At the same time, there is and can be no requirement that the applicant describe or predict every possible means of accomplishing that function.[104]

The implication that functional language would cover every possible means of accomplishing the function was repeated in several other decisions.[105] This language was interpreted by the patent bar as broadening the scope of functional language in claims.

After these early decisions, the pendulum swung back. In 1989 in *Johnston v. IVAC Corp.*, the Federal Circuit again used sweeping language, this time on the opposite end of the arc:

> [A requirement] in a claim described as a means for performing a function, if read literally, would encompass any means for performing the function. But Sections 112 [par.] 6 operates to *cut back* [emphasis added] on the type of means which could literally satisfy the claim language.[106]

Thus, users of functional claim language bear the risk of that language being narrowly interpreted. This decision further remarked that literal infringement was not present unless the same function is found in the accused device.[107] The dictates

Legal Focus
continued

of *Johnston* were followed in several Federal Circuit decisions.[108] If the logic encompassed in these cases wins out, then the death of functional claims language is not far off. However, the Federal Circuit itself continues to struggle with where to draw the line on functional language.[109]

The use of functional language in a claim necessarily results in the question: What does such language cover? The possibilities range from any structure which can produce the described function to only that specific structure described in the patent. Congress itself provided guidance about this issue, drawing the line between these two extremes. "Such a claim shall be construed to cover the corresponding structure, material, or acts described in the perforation *and equivalents thereof* [emphasis added]."[110] Unfortunately, Congress relied on the term "equivalent" in defining this line. The use of this term was unfortunate because of confusion with the doctrine of equivalents. Under the doctrine of equivalents, even if a claim does not literally read on an accused device, infringement can be found.[111] (See Doctrine of Equivalents, above.) Under the Supreme Court's recent pronouncement of this doctrine, "a product or process that does not literally infringe upon the express terms of a patent claim may nonetheless be found to infringe" if "insubstantial differences" exist between the claims and the accused product.[112]

The coexisting use of the term "equivalents" to describe two distinct concepts has led to confusion about the scope of functional claim language. While the Supreme Court recently gave guidance on the doctrine of equivalents, the scope of functional claim language needs clarification. In the 1997 decision of *Warner-Jenkinson v. Hilton Davis*, the issue was whether a narrowing claim amendment, apparently not required to distinguish over the prior art, could expand under the doctrine of equivalents. The Supreme Court decided the reason for the amendment must be examined, with only amendments made to avoid the prior art limiting the expansion of the claim language under the doctrine of equivalents.

Thus, while not specifically ruling on the issue of functional language in claims, the Supreme Court endorsed the doctrine of equivalents. In view of this endorsement, it is difficult to believe the specific application of the doctrine of equivalents, including the application to functional language, is on the downswing.

With courts swinging back and forth in interpreting the scope of functional language, the law as interpreted by the Ninth Circuit in 1944, which Congress explicitly endorsed by overruling the *Halliburton* case, should be considered. The functional language was a means for tuning a receiver to the frequency of a particular echo to distinguish from other echoes.[113] The patent described a mechanical acoustical resonator as the structure behind this language. The accused infringer employed an electronic filter.

The Ninth Circuit ruled that the electronic filter was within the scope of the claim under the doctrine of equivalents. In addition, the Appeals Court concluded the electronic filter was not a literal equivalent, but that it performed "substantially the same function in substantially the same way to obtain substantially the same result" under the doctrine of equivalents.

When interpreting functional language, the first step is to determine the literal scope of the claims.[114] The critical inquiry is whether the accused device performs the exact function of the claim requirement by use of a technical equivalent. Technical equivalency requires an insubstantial change that adds nothing of significance to the structure, material, or acts described in the specification. In determining literal infringement, the specification, the prosecution history, other claims in the patent, and expert testimony should be considered; however, an analysis of the prior art is not needed.

After the literal scope of the functional language is determined, the second step is to determine whether this scope could be expanded under a standard doctrine of equivalents analysis. This is for the jury, not the judge to decide. In contrast to the inquiry regarding the technical equivalency, the doctrine of equivalents determines the legal equivalency. In determining legal equivalency, the function must be substantially the same, but need not be identical. In addition, the value of the significance of the invention in the context of the prior art should be considered, with minor inventions in crowded technologies given a narrow scope of legal equivalents and pioneer inventions given a broad scope of legal equivalents.[115]

Recent cases may well have redefined where the line is drawn for functional language: between literal infringement and infringement under the doctrine of equivalents. It is risky to read as a net result the narrowing of the metes and bounds of functional language. Until the law is settled in this area, entrepreneurial managers should be cautious in making business decisions relying on narrowly interpreting functional language.[116] Otherwise, the comfort currently derived by focusing on specific descriptions of structure in narrowly interpreting functional language could well lead to greater discomfort later on.

## Endnotes

1. *Patents*, Title 35, U.S. Code §271.

2. Ibid., §154a.

3. Ibid., §§154b, 156.

4. Ibid., §101.

5. Ibid., §§102, 103.

6. *Bonito Boat, Inc. v. Thunder Craft Boats, Inc.*, 489 U.S. 141, 150 (1989).

7. *Graham v. John Deere Co.*, 383 U.S. 1, 17–18 (1966).

8. *Patents*, Title 35, §101.

9. *Brenner v. Manson*, 383 U.S. 519 (1966).

10. *Campbell v. Wettstein*, 476 F. 2d 642 (C.C.P.A. 1973).

11. *Gottschalk v. Benson*, 409 U.S. 63 (1972); *Parker v. Flook*, 437 U.S. 584 (1978).

12. *Patents*, Title 35, §101.

13. *Diamond v. Chakrabarty*, 447 U.S. 303 (1981).

14. *Diamond v. Diehr*, 450 U.S. 175 (1981).

15. Len Kleinrock, "Information Flow in Large Communications Nets," *Massachusetts Insitutue of Technology Research Laboratory of Electronics (R.L.E.) Quarterly Progress Report* (1960); and Paul Baren, "On Distributed Communications Networks," *Institute of Electronics and Electrical Engineers (I.E.E.E.) Transactions on Systems* (March 1964).

16. *Gottschalk v. Benson*.

17. *Parker v. Flook*, 437 U.S. 584 (1978).

18. Vincent Cerf and Robert Kahn, "A Protocol for Packet Network Intercommunication," *I.E.E.E. Transactions on Communications Technology* (May 1974).

19. *Diamond v. Diehr*.

20. *In re Iwahashi*, 888 F. 2d 1370 (Fed. Cir. 1989).

21. *Arrhythmia Research Technology, Inc. v. Corazonix Corp.*, 958 F. 2d 1053 (Fed. Cir. 1992).

22. *In re Alappat*, 33 F. 3d 1526 (Fed. Cir. 1994).

23. *State Street Bank and Trust Co. v. Signature Financial Group, Inc.*, 149 F. 3d 1368 (Fed. Cir. 1999).

24. *Patents*, Title 35, §102.

25. Ibid.

26. *City of Elizabeth v. American Nicholson Pavement Co.*, 97 U.S. 126 (1878).

27. *Coleman v. Dines*, 754 F. 2d 353, 359 (Fed. Cir. 1985).

28. *Patents*, Title 35, §135.

29. Ibid., §171.

30. Ibid., §§161, 163.

31. Ibid., §120.

32. Ibid.

33. Ibid., §121.

34. Ibid.

35. Ibid., §§301–307.

36. Ibid., §251.

37. Ibid., §112.

38. *In re Lundak*, 773 F. 2d 1216 (Fed. Cir. 1985).

39. *Copyrights*, Title 17, U.S. CODE, §901.

40. *Patents*, Title 35, §112.

41. Ibid., §271a.

42. Ibid., §112.

43. *Standard Oil Company v. American Cyanamid Company*, 774 F. 2d 448 (Fed. Cir. 1985).

44. *Warner-Jenkinson Co., Inc. v. Hilton Davis Chemical Co.*, 520 U.S. 17 (1997).

45. *Ex parte Jepson*, 1917 Comm. Dec. 62 (Asst' Comr Pat. 1917).

46. *Warner-Jenkinson v. Hilton Davis*, 520.

47. *McGill v. John Zink Co.*, 736 F. 2d 666 (Fed. Cir. 1989).

48. *Graver Tank & Manufacturing Company v. Linde Air Products Company*, 339 U.S. 605 (1950); *Warner-Jenkinson v. Hilton Davis*.

49. *Standard Oil v. American Cyanamid*.

50. *Graver Tank v. Linde Air Products*.

51. *Atlas Powder Co. v. E.I. DuPont de Nemours & Co.*, 750 F. 2d 1569,1580 (Fed. Cir. 1984).

52. *Rolls-Royce, Ltd. v. GTE Valeron Corp.*, 800 F. 2d 1101, 1110 n.9 (Fed. Cir. 1986).

53. *Patents*, Title 35, §282.

54. *Stratoflex, Inc. v. Aerogroup Corp.*, 713 F. 2d 1530, 1534 (Fed. Cir. 1983).

55. *Pfaff v. Wells Electronics, Inc.*, 525 U.S. 55 (1998).

56. *Marconi Wireless Telegraph Co. v. DeForest Radio, Telephone & Telegraph Co.*, 243 F. 560 (2d Cir. 1917).

57. *Funk Bros. Seed v. Kalo Inoculate*, 333 U.S. 127 (1948).

58. *Diamond v. Chakrabarty*, 447 U.S. 303 (1980).

59. Ibid., 30.

60. *In re Allen*, 2 U.S.P.Q. 2d 1425 (Bd. Pat. App. and Interf. 1987).

61. *Federal Courts Improvement Act of 1982*, 96 Stat. 25. *Courts of Appeal*, Title 28, U.S. CODE, §1295.

62. *Federal Courts Improvement Act*, Public Law 275, 97th Cong., 1st sess., (1981), H. Rept. 312.

63. Ibid.

64. Ibid., 20–23.

65. In *Eli Lilly & Co. v. Medtronic, Inc.*, 496 U.S. 661 (1990), the Court ruled that medical devices as well as drugs were covered by the Drug Price Competition and Patent Term Restoration Act; and in *Cardinal Chemical Company v. Morton International, Inc.*, 508 U.S. 83 (1993), the Court rejected the practice of the Federal Circuit of vacating findings of invalidity as moot when it found a patent not infringed, based on the public policy of invalidating bad patents. In addition to these two cases, the Supreme Court decided two cases related to but not on patent issues and one appeal from the Third Circuit Court of Appeals. In *Bonito Boats v. Thunder Craft Boats*, the Court held that a Florida law prohibiting use of direct molded duplication of boat hulls was preempted by the patent laws. In *Asgrow Seed Co. v. Winterboer*, 513 U.S. 179 (1995), the Court ruled on the Plant Variety Protection Act. In *General Motors Corp. v. Devex Corp.*, 461 U.S. 648 (1983), the Court affirmed the Third Circuit in deciding that prejudgment interest should ordinarily be awarded when a patent is infringed.

66. *Dickinson v. Zurko*, 119 S.Ct. 1816 (1999).

67. *Patents*, Title 35, §102b.

68. *Pfaff v. Wells Electronics, Inc.*, 525 U.S. 55 (1998).

69. *Pfaff v. Wells Electronics, Inc.*, 9 U.S.P.Q. 2d 1366 (N.D. Ind. 1988).

70. *Pfaff v. Wells Electronics, Inc.*, 124 F. 3d 1429 (Fed. Cir. 1997).

71. Ibid., 1433.

72. Ibid., 1433, citing *Micro Chemical, Inc. v. Great Plains Chemical Co.*, 103 F. 3d 1538, 1544 (Fed. Cir. 1997); *UMC Electronics Co. v. United States*, 816 F. 2d 647, 656 (Fed. Cir.1987).

73. *Pfaff v. Wells Electronics, Inc.*, 525 U.S. 67.

74. Ibid.

75. Ibid., 63, citing *Timely Products, Corp. v. Arron*, 523 F. 2d 288 (2d Cir. 1975) and *Dart Industries, Inc. v. E.I. DuPont de Nemours & Co.*, 489 F. 2d 1359 (7th Cir. 1973), *cert. denied*, 17 U.S. 933 (1979).

76. *Cardinal Chemical Co. v. Morton International, Inc.*, 508 U.S. 83, 91 (1993).

77. *Warner-Jenkins Co., Inc. v. Hilton Davis Chemical Co.*, 520 U.S. 17 (1997).

78. "We concur with [Judge Nies'] apt reconciliation of our two lines of precedent." 525 U.S. 57.

79. *Warner-Jenkinson Co., Inc. v. Hilton Davis Chemical Co.*, 62 F. 3d 1512, 1521–1522 (Fed. Cir. 1995).

80. Ibid., 1537–38.

81. Ibid., 1574.

82. *Warner-Jenkinson v. Hilton Davis*, 520 U.S. 26.

83. Ibid., 29.

84. Has the Federal Circuit gotten the message? Perhaps not, as shown by the recent decision in *Festo Corp. v. Shoketsu Kinzoku Kogyo Kabushiki Co., Ltd.*, 243 F. 3d 558 (Fed. Cir. 2000), in which the doctrine once again was severely cut back.

85. *Markman v. Westview Instruments, Inc.*, 517 U.S. 370 (1996).

86. *Markman v. Westview Instruments, Inc.*, 772 F. Supp. 1535, (E.D. Pa. 1991).

87. *Markman v. Westview Instruments, Inc.*, 52 F. 3d 967 (Fed. Cir. 1995).

88. *State Street v. Signature Financial.*

89. *B. Braun Medical Inc. v. Abbott Laboratories*, 124 F. 3d 1419 (Fed. Cir. 1998).

90. *Festo Corp. v. Shoketsu*; and *Dawn Equipment v. Kentucky Farms*, 140 F. 3d 1009 (Fed. Cir. 1998).

91. *Fina Research, S.A. v. Baroid Limited*, 141 F. 3d 1479 (Fed. Cir. 1998).

92. *Nobelpharma A.B. v. Implant Innovations, Inc.*, 129 F. 3d 1463 (Fed. Cir. 1997).

93. *Standard Oil v. American Cyanamid.*

94. *O'Reilly v. Morse*, 56 U.S. 62 (1854).

95. *Holland Furniture Co. v. Perkins Glue Co.*, 277 U.S. 245 (1928); and *General Electric Co. v. Wabash Appliance Co.*, 304 U.S. 364 (1938).

96. *Continental Paper Bag Co. v. Eastern Paper Bag Co.*, 210 U.S. 405 (1881).

97. *Halliburton Oil Well Cementing Co. v. Walker*, 329 U.S. 1 (1946).

98. *Halliburton Oil Well Cementing Co. v. Walker*, 146 F. 2d 817 (9th Cir. 1944), *reversed*, 329 U.S. 1 (1946).

99. *Patents*, Title 35, §112, ¶6.

100. *In re Hyatt*, 708 F. 2d 712 (Fed. Cir. 1983).

101. *Patents*, Title 35, §112, ¶1; and *In re Hayes Micro Computer Products Inc. Patent Litigation*, 982 F. 2d 1527, 1535 (Fed. Cir. 1992).

102. *Patents*, Title 35, §112, ¶2.

103. *Court of Appeal*, Title 28, U.S. CODE, §1295.

104. *D.M.I., Inc. v. Deere & Co.*, 755 F. 2d 1570, 1579 (Fed. Cir. 1985).

105. *P.M. Palumbo v. Don-Joy Co.*, 762 F. 2d 969, 974 (Fed. Cir. 1985); *King Instruments Corp. v. Otari Corp.*, 767 F. 2d 853, 862 (Fed. Cir. 1985), *cert. denied*, 475 U.S. 1016 (1986).

106. *Johnston v. IVAC Corp.*, 885 F. 2d 1574, 1580 (Fed. Cir. 1989).

107. Ibid.

108. *Jonsson v. Stanley Works*, 903 F. 2d 812 (Fed. Cir. 1990); and *Valmont v. Reinke*, 983 F. 2d 1039 (Fed. Cir. 1993).

109. Philip Kotler, *Marketing Management*, 6th ed. (Scarborough, Ontario: Prentice-Hall Canada, 1989), 468.

110. *Patents*, Title 35, §112, ¶6.

111. *Graver Tank & Mfg. Co. v. Linde Air Products Co.*, 339 U.S. 605 (1950).

112. *Warner-Jenkinson v. Hilton Davis*, 520 U.S. 31.

113. *Halliburton v. Walker*, 329 U.S. 9.

114. *Markman v. Westview Instruments, Inc.*, 517 U.S. 370 (1996).

115. *Hughes Aircraft Co. v. United States.*, 717 F. 2d 135, 1362 (Fed. Cir. 1983); *Chemical Engineering Corp. v. Essef Industries, Inc.*, 795 F. 2d 1565, 1572 n.8 (Fed. Cir. 1984).

116. The controversy continues. In *Dawn Equipment Co. v. Kentucky Farms Inc.*, 186 F. 3d 981 (Fed. Cir. 1998), each member of the three-panel court issued a separate opinion on the issue of equivalents. Judge S. Jay Plager questioned whether equivalents under the statute (*Patents*, Title 35, §112, ¶6) should be different than equivalents under the doctrine of equivalents; Judge Pauline Newman defended the well-understood distinction between these equivalents; and Judge Paul Michael questioned whether expanding the scope of functional language under the doctrine of equivalents conflicts with the statute.

## Chapter 3

# BRANDING AND TRADEMARKS

**Branding**

**Due**

**Diligence**

Despite tentatively naming his company Marvin Enterprises, George already had misgivings about this name. Too often, the name of the company is chosen with little or no thought, often based on a symbolic connection to the founders. To avoid expending attention and resources on the name after success is achieved, our entrepreneurs should immediately resolve several naming issues. Do they want to use the name to assist in marketing the product? Do they want to convey to customers the type of company and rely on brand names to market the product?

Thus, George called a meeting to reassess the name of the new company and the new product, and it went something like this:

George Marvin: I've been reading up on branding strategies in the consumer electronics area and I think we need to reassess the name of our company and the name of the product. I was thinking of having an internal competition with a reward for whomever's name suggestion is chosen.

Chip Norton: Why don't we just stick to "gargle-blaster?"

Mildred Marvin: Bad idea. I never liked that name. I was reading an article about a firm in New York that uses a computer to invent names for products. It would be neat to use them.

George: I used a naming firm when I was with BigCo and it cost big bucks. Additionally, we just don't have the marketing resources to develop name recognition for an invented new name. We need a name that will sell the product.

Mildred: Well, whatever we do, XYZ Competitive Company is just going to use the same or a similar name on their copycat product. Even if we can prevent XYZ from copying our products, they'll just imitate our marketing and end up stealing away all our customers. I'm sick and tired of this, and I want to put a stop to it with this product!

The branding strategy for the product also relates to the naming of the company. Does George wish to develop a distinctive name for more than one product, for example, across a product line? Do our entrepreneurs wish to designate individual products within the product line by a generic name, a numerical designation, or even a descriptive name? Do they wish to develop a family of marks that share a common feature which can be used to build on previously established consumer recognition?

Essentially, trademark due diligence entails two stages:

▶ Does use of the company or brand name infringe on any third party rights?

▶ What is the potential strength of the trademark?

Again, because most intellectual property extends only within national boundaries, appropriate due diligence should be directed to each country where significant product sales will occur. Branding due diligence often raises unique questions in foreign countries. For example, if the trademark is to be used in non-English-speaking countries, the meaning of the word — or closely related words — in the host language should be investigated.

Infamous faux pas in this realm of American marketers include:

▶ Coors' translation of its slogan, "Turn it loose," into Spanish, where it read "Suffer from diarrhea."

▶ Clairol's introduction of its curling iron "Mist Stick" in Germany, where "mist" is slang for manure.

▶ Pepsi's "Come alive with the Pepsi Generation" translated into "Pepsi brings your ancestors back from the grave" in Chinese.

▶ Frank Perdue's chicken slogan, "it takes a strong man to make a tender chicken" translated into Spanish as "it takes an aroused man to make a chicken affectionate."

▶ The Coca-Cola name in China was first read as "Ke-kou-ke-la," meaning "Bite the wax tadpole" or "female horse stuffed with wax," depending on the dialect.

Even if closely related words have inoffensive meanings, are their cultural implications related to the context of the product? If the name is an arbitrary term such as Apple computers, should the English "apple" or the word in the host language for apple be used?

In stage one due diligence, the availability of the name should be explored and understood. An independent survey of uses of similar marks should be conducted to identify potential conflicts. If the company does not own the brand name, but has accessed rights by license, an understanding of the licensed rights is essential. The barrier such license provides varies from an exclusive licensee (which is tantamount to ownership) to nonexclusive. The financial impact of any royalty payments should be included as an additional cost-of-goods sold. Finally, any limitations placed in the licensed rights — such as a limited field of use license — should be understood, particularly if the company plans on extending the brand name beyond the current product line.

In stage two due diligence, the strength of the trademark should be explored. The strength greatly depends on the type of word used as a trademark. The existence of similar brand names on related goods also affects the strength of the trademark. Therefore, the survey of related uses of similar marks should be reviewed to understand the strength of the trademark.

## The Coffee Wars

In most urban markets, a Starbucks coffeehouse is found at nearly every corner. From its humble start in Seattle, Starbucks has grown into a huge enterprise with coffeehouses across the United States as well as in Canada, Japan, the Philippines, Taiwan, Thailand, New Zealand, Malaysia, the United Kingdom, China, and Kuwait. However, the history of Starbucks and a rival coffee shop with a remarkably similar origin demonstrates the importance of avoiding conflicts in naming a new product. Without several miscues, one can only wonder if the ubiquitous coffeehouse on each corner could have been that rival.

The first Starbucks opened in 1971 in Pike Place Market — Seattle's legendary open-air farmer's market — as Starbucks' Coffee, Tea & Spices. The growth of Starbucks followed the 1985 purchase of the company by Starbucks' director of retail operations, Howard Schultz. By 1993, Starbucks was a publicly-owned company. Starbucks has now grown to more than 2,200 stores.

Three years prior to that first Starbucks, Jim Stewart opened the Wet Whisker in Coupeville on Whidbey Island, Washington. The Wet Whisker was a combination coffee and ice cream shop. With expansion in mind, this store was sold to a local family in 1970. Stewart then opened a store called Stewart Brothers Coffee on Pier 70 on Seattle's waterfront. This store likewise featured coffee and ice cream. Shortly before the opening of Starbucks' Coffee, Tea & Spices, Stewart opened a retail store in Pike Place Market.

Unfortunately for Stewart, Stewarts Private Blend Foods, Inc., a retail coffee brand in the Midwest, had used "Stewarts" as a brand name for coffee since 1914. Stewarts Private Blend registered "Stewarts" for coffee as U.S. Trademark Registration 1,054,039 in 1976. In response, Stewart dropped his use of the name Stewart, shortening the name to SBC, the acronym for Stewart Brothers Coffee. Later that year, he began referring to the shops as Seattle's Best Coffee, based on the acronym SBC and his success in winning a Seattle coffee taste-off. Thus, within the span of 20 years, the business used no fewer than four brand names: the Wet Whisker, Stewart Brothers Coffee, SBC, and Seattle's Best Coffee. It is of course left to speculation what the end result of the coffeehouse wars might have been without these missteps in branding.

CASE

STUDY

CONT.

---

# An Overview of the Trademark Laws

By playing a role in several new product introductions before returning to business school, George had sympathy for the Zen-like issues marketers faced in branding. Every time the marketers came up with a mark that would sell the product, the trademark attorneys would nix it, claiming the mark could not be protected. George had less sympathy for the trademark attorneys. He often wondered if the trademark attorneys would rather randomly assign a word out of the dictionary to brand the product. George knew that to entrepreneurially manage his company, he had to take an active role in branding as he did in financing and marketing, taking advice from the experts but ultimately making the decisions himself.

## What Are Trademarks?

Trademarks refer to those words, slogans, designs, and other symbols used to identify and distinguish the goods or services of a business from the goods and services of other businesses. In branding, two areas of legal focus are critical. The legal scope of the term to be used as a brand name will determine the strength of the trademark throughout the product's life. In addition, a realistic branding strategy that recognizes the available marketing resources and corporate culture is essential. By understanding and focusing on these legal implications of branding, entrepreneurial managers can make better branding decisions. (For a description of the process and costs of filing a trademark application, see Appendix B.)

When naming a product, the function on which managers focus is use of the brand name as an instrument in selling the products.[1] This function can conflict with other considerations that can haunt the brand manager long after a brand name is chosen. Branding decisions made years earlier affect the degree to which others can be prevented from using offensively similar brand names on similar goods long after immeasurable time, effort, and money have been invested in promoting the brand.

Management's lack of understanding of the legal implications of branding is in large part due to the lack of communication between managers and those responsible for interpreting and offering counsel on the law, that is, attorneys. In branding, attorneys and marketers cannot even agree on their terminology. Attorneys generally do not use the designations "branding," "brand," or "brand name." For example, leading legal commentators identify brand name as a colloquial way to refer to a trademark.[2] On the other hand, a leading marketing expert defines brand name as the identification given to a product and trademark as a legally protectable brand name.[3] This distinction, a lawyer would argue, is faulty because a nonprotectable identification of a product is free for all to use and thus not a brand name at all. The terms brand name and brand will be used here except when legal context suggests the use of the term trademark.

The laws of the United States define a trademark as "... any word, name, symbol or device or any combination thereof adopted and used by a manufacturer or merchant to identify his goods and distinguish them from those manufactured or sold by others."[4] Trade names are the words, slogans, designs, and other symbols used to distinguish a business or company from the business of others.[5] The same word can be used in both the trade name and the trademark sense, such as when the Xerox Corporation sells Xerox copiers.

## Other Types of Branding

The law also recognizes other types of brand names. Service marks are words, slogans, designs, and other symbols used to distinguish services from those of others.[6] While most uses of service marks are clear, this area can seemingly overlap trademark usage, such as McDonald's Corporation's registration of Egg McMuffin as a service mark for serving the breakfast sandwich.[7]

Certification marks are used to certify those goods or services that meet standards set by the certifier.[8] The common designation "UL Approved" is an example of a certification mark.[9] Collective marks are used to indicate membership in an organization.[10] The Professional Golfers Association or PGA is an example of a collective mark.[11]

# Unfair Competition

Unfair competition is a broad concept that encompasses trademark protection. In addition to trademarks, unfair competition includes:

> ► Trade dress — the impression given by the product and packaging as a whole.[12]

► False or misleading advertising.[13]

► Misappropriation of trade secrets.[14]

► Dilution, which protects famous trademarks from a "gradual whittling away" of the strength of a brand name by a third party's nonconfusing use.[15]

► Trade disparagement, which protects against disparagement of products or services.[16]

► Trade libel, which protects against maligning the integrity of a business.[17]

While trademark law is directed towards the use of words, slogans, designs, and other symbols, trade dress governs the impression given by the product and packaging as a whole. This broad category includes the impression given by labels and even the look of the product itself. For example, the look of greeting cards could be protected as trade dress. Because the facts to show trademark infringement are substantially the same as the facts to show trade dress infringement, both claims often are presented in the same lawsuit.

Like trademark protection, trade dress protection does not cover functional aspects of products or labels. Protection of functional aspects of products is left to patents and trade secrets. Trade dress also does not encompass vague or abstract product images and generally does not encompass marketing themes. Thus, Häagen-Dazs was unsuccessful in stopping Frusen Glädjé's imitation of its successful Scandinavian marketing theme for ice cream.[18] (See Case Study: Nonprotectable Trade "Marketing," below.)

## Nonprotectable Trade "Marketing"

Despite the breadth of trade dress protection, the tenet of free competition sometimes wins out. The story of Häagen-Dazs is an apt illustration of a wildly successful marketing scheme imitated by competitors. Made in Woodbridge, New Jersey, Häagen Dazs' only connection to Scandinavia was the made-up name and the map on the packaging.

The story of Häagen-Dazs begins with Senator, a small, family-owned company in New York whose roots extend back to the 1920s. In the 1950s, large manufacturing concerns like Kraft and Borden successfully consolidated and nationalized the ice cream market. This squeezed local ice cream companies like Senator. To reduce production costs, the national brands reduced the amount of butter fat to federally mandated minimums, added chemical stabilizers, and, in a process called "aeration," whipped up the volume of their product.

Reuben and Rose Mattus, the owners of Senator, responded with a classic niche-marketing scheme — rich, calorie-laden ice cream made from real egg yolks and cream and aimed at high-end consumers. Most importantly, the product used no

CASE

STUDY

CONT.

aeration. Mattus gave the product a Danish-sounding name — which doesn't mean anything in the Danish language — because a family friend returning from a European trip bragged about a rich ice cream sold in Denmark. Despite a 75-percent cost premium over the national brands, the product jumped off Manhattan delicatessen and neighborhood store shelves. Incredibly, with no advertising, no overall marketing strategy, and volunteer distribution of the product, a near-national presence was established by the late 1970s.

The success of Häagen-Dazs spawned competition in the premium ice cream niche. This competition included an entry named Frusen Glädjé, which means "frozen delight" in Swedish. Industry giant Dolly Madison, working in conjunction with Edward Lipitz, introduced Frusen Glädjé. Not coincidentally, Lipitz was Mattus' cousin and a former Häagen-Dazs distributor.

In 1980, Häagen-Dazs sued Frusen Glädjé. Häagen-Dazs claimed Frusen Glädjé copied Häagen-Dazs' "unique Scandinavia marketing theme" in its product in such a way as to "cash in on the commercial magnetism of the exclusive marketing technique developed . . . by the family which owns and operates Häagen-Dazs."[19]

Häagen-Dazs' lawyers specifically identified five features of Frusen Glädjé's packaging they claimed were taken from Häagen-Dazs' packaging and confused purchasers:

- ▶ The phraseology used in reciting the ingredients of the product.
- ▶ A recitation of the artificial ingredients not found in the product.
- ▶ Instructions on the manner in which the product was to be eaten to enhance flavor.
- ▶ A two word Germanic-sounding name having an umlaut over the letter "a."
- ▶ A map of Scandinavia.[20]

The court was not impressed. Finding the products actually bore little physical resemblance, the court decided Häagen-Dazs' "unique Scandinavia marketing theme" was not protectable in the absence of a likelihood of confusion, which was dispelled by the dissimilarity in the product's image. Few tears should be shed for the Mattuses. In 1984, with sales at the family-owned company reaching $100 million, Mattus sold out to industry giant Pillsbury for $76 million.

## Free Competition

Entrepreneurial managers understand the economic backdrop underlying the laws of unfair competition. A fundamental building block of the economic system of the United States is free competition.[21] Unfettered free competition, however, would mean any competitor could freely copy not only the functionality of products, but also any brand name, company name, trade dress, or packaging. The resulting consumer confusion is difficult to imagine. Thus, for brand names, as in many areas of economic competition, free competition is regulated.

In imitating or copying materials freely available to the public, the regulation of free competition occurs by carving out specific categories where such competition is not permitted, such as patents and copyrights, in addition to the categories of unfair competition. In the absence of a product, name, idea, or product image fitting into such a category, it should, according to public policy, be free to copy. It is the courts, with the general guidance of Congress, who referee what fits into these categories.

## The View of the Courts

Unlike managers, who focus on how brand names help sell goods, courts are concerned with other aspects of brand names.[22] When we hear the name of a person with whom we are familiar, that name embodies our experience with and the reputation of that person. Likewise, courts view a brand name as embodying the reputation of the goods to which it is attached. This reputation is part of the goodwill of the product.[23] Legally, this symbolic representation serves three roles:

- ▸ Helps distinguish a brand owner's goods from those of competitors.[24]
- ▸ Groups goods bearing a mark as coming from a single — but possibly anonymous — source.[25]
- ▸ Signals these goods will be of comparable quality to other goods bearing the brand name.[26]

Brand names chosen with only the sales function in mind can fall short in characteristics that affect these roles.

Once equity in a brand name has been established, managers doubtless view their brand names as a property right. When a brand owner authorizes his attorney to sue an offending user of a similar brand name, that owner is primarily concerned with the competitor gaining an economic benefit to which the brand owner feels entitled. While such natural rights considerations can play a role, the court's primary consideration is protecting the consuming public from confusion.[27] Thus, in a very real sense the laws of unfair competition are consumer-protection laws. The brand name owner's right to sell to a nonconfused public aligns the interest of the brand owner with the interest of consumers.[28]

Additionally, while a brand name owner may feel ownership in a form of property, the analogy of trademark rights to real property rights is tenuous. For trademarks to be analogous to real property, real property rights would have to be radically different. For instance, the scope of the property would be defined not by a deed as in real property — or even by claims as in a patent — but rather by the public perception of the property. Were this true, property owners would need to take affirmative steps to maintain the proper public perception, such as clear labeling of the bounds of the property, diligence in policing the public's use of the property, and education of the public about the proper bounds of the property.

For brand names, the owner should indeed take such affirmative steps to maintain the public's perception of the owner's rights. For example, a brand owner cannot transfer the trademark without also transferring the goodwill it represents. This concept can be violated when the trademark transferee does not use the brand name on goods having substantially the same characteristics as the seller's goods.[29] In addition, a brand owner must retain control of the quality of goods on which a trademark is licensed.[30] The brand owner should police offending uses by others to preserve the rights established in the trademark. The manager also must realize that, unlike real property or patents, a brand name owner cannot exclude all use of his brand name: for example, nonconfusing forms of comparative advertising. The only uses the owner can exclude are those likely to lead to consumer confusion.

## Branding Qualifications

What then qualify as the words, slogans, designs, and other symbols used to distinguish goods or services from others? Words are clearly capable of achieving trademark status. Abbreviations such as VW[31] or numbers such as Channel No. 5[32] have achieved trademark status. Phrases such as "Hair Color So Natural Only Her Hairdresser Knows For Sure"[33] have achieved trademark status, also. Nicknames such as Hog (for motorcycle)[34] and Bug (for automobile)[35] have achieved cult as well as trademark status.

Symbols can achieve trademark status. Examples include Levi's pocket tab[36] and back pocket stitching design,[37] Adidas' three stripes,[38] and the Dallas Cowboy Cheerleader uniforms[39] (see Case Study: Protectable Trade "Dress," below). Product configuration examples include the green Perrier Indian Club-shaped bottle,[40] the Coca-Cola Bottle,[41] the silhouette shape of the classic Weber grill,[42] and the front grille of a Rolls-Royce automobile.[43] The original golden arches of McDonald's building configuration[44] and the Fotomat kiosk[45] are examples of building structures recognized as trademarks. Yellow taxi cabs[46] and pink fiberglass insulation[47] have trademark recognition. Even the National Broadcasting Company's familiar three-note chime achieved trademark status.[48]

These examples demonstrate the wide range of available words, slogans, designs, and symbols that can distinguish goods or services. These examples also demonstrate the gray area between trademarks and trade dress that, because of the similarity in proving infringement, is usually a distinction without significance. These symbols qualify as trademarks, not because managers or their attorneys intended them to, but because they are source-indicative in the minds of consumers.

## Protectable Trade "Dress"

A strange example demonstrates the breadth of this type of intellectual property. America's sweethearts, the Dallas Cowboy Cheerleaders, first made their appearance in 1972 when Tex Schramm recognized that professional football was more than sport — it was entertainment. While loved by fans at Texas Stadium, it wasn't until 1976 that Dallas Cowboy Cheerleaders got their national break. During a lull in the action of Super Bowl X, a television cameraman brought their live routine into 75 million homes. The next season their fame exploded, stimulated by appearances on two network television specials and climaxing with a 1979 made-for-television movie, *The Dallas Cowboy Cheerleaders*.

The Dallas Cowboy Cheerleader uniforms have remained essentially the same since their introduction in 1972: in May 1989, western-styled boots replaced the original go-go boots; in 1991, low-cut shorts replaced a large-buckled belt; in 1992, traditional cowboy boots replaced the western-styled boots; in 1993, the 15 states on the uniform were outlined by crystals; and in 1994, a more western lapel was added to the blouse.

Thousands of miles away, the name of Michael Zaffarano's movie theater in New York City — "Pussycat Cinema" — left little doubt of the content of the movies. In November 1978, Zaffarano ran a movie titled *Debbie Does Dallas*, which depicted a cheerleader in a fictional high school who has been selected to become a "Texas Cowgirl." To raise money to go to Dallas, Debbie performs sexual services for a fee. The majority of the movie consists of scenes graphically depicting the sexual escapades of the actors. In the movie's final scene, Debbie dons a uniform strikingly similar to the Dallas Cowboy Cheerleader uniforms. For approximately twelve minutes, Debbie engages in various sex acts while partially clad in the uniform. Advertisements for the movie showed Debbie in the uniform and — even though the actress had never been a Dallas Cowboy Cheerleader — included the tag line, "You'll do more than cheer for this X Dallas Cheerleader."

Not amused, the Dallas Cowboy Cheerleaders, Inc. sued. Zaffarano argued the Dallas Cowboy Cheerleaders' uniforms were purely functional items necessary for performing the cheerleading routines and therefore not protectable. The judge rejected this defense, perhaps influenced by the content of the movie, which he or she called "sexually depraved." The court found the western flavor of the uniforms, embodied in the particular combination of colors and decorations, protectable.

## Consumer Recognition

For many nonword trademarks, developing consumer recognition is difficult, expensive, and time consuming. The value of these trademarks often lies in stopping intentional creation of consumer confusion.[49] Because of their primary importance, our focus is brand names.

It is important to note that the standard applied for a court to step in and stop someone from using a brand name does not require proof of actual confusion. Rather, the standard is whether someone's use of a brand name is likely to cause confusion, cause mistake, or deceive an appreciable number of consumers.[50] Several important concepts are built into this standard.

Confusion refers not only to the source of a product but to affiliation with, connection to, or sponsorship of the product. In addition, courts differ considerably about what makes up an appreciable number of consumers. Survey evidence showing confusion in as low as eight percent of consumers has met this standard,[51] although consumer confusion this low does not require a finding of likelihood of confusion. The consumer has been identified as a normal purchaser buying with ordinary caution.[52]

Because judges obviously cannot read the minds of these hypothetical consumers, a different approach is taken in deciding whether a likelihood of confusion exists. While different courts use different terms, the general approach followed is:

- ► comparing the similarity of the brand name;
- ► comparing the similarity of the goods or services;
- ► determining the conditions under which the goods or services are purchased, including the distribution channels and the sophistication of the purchaser;
- ► determining the strength of the brand name; and
- ► considering any available objective evidence, such as evidence of confusion or deliberate copying.[53]

No single factor is determinative and every case is examined in light of its particular facts. Nevertheless, entrepreneurial managers can gain intuition into the branding process by understanding these factors.

### Comparing the Similarity of Brand Names

Initially, the court will consider the similarity between the brand names in determining whether a likelihood of confusion exists. The three primary inquiries are comparison of the sight, sound, and meaning.[54] Because the sight test is the principal test for nonword marks, the focus for brand names is sound and meaning. In this area, examples are worth a thousand words; brand names found to be confusingly similar in sound include:

- ▶ ESSO versus S.O.[55]
- ▶ Dramamine versus Bonamine[56]
- ▶ Coca-Cola versus Cup-O'Cola[57]
- ▶ Jockey versus Rocke[58]

Brand names found to be confusingly similar in meaning include:

- ▶ Pledge versus Promise[59]
- ▶ Blue Nun versus Blue Angel[60]
- ▶ Black Cat versus Chat Noir[61]

The last example shows the rule that foreign words are generally translated into English to decide whether confusion is likely.

## Comparing the Similarity of Goods or Services

It is not required that the goods be identical or even compete. Rather, if a brand name is likely to cause confusion, even if used on noncompetitive goods, infringement exists. Use of similar brand names on different but related goods, if such related goods are within the likely realm of product-line extensions, is often likely to cause confusion. For example, use of the brand name Black & White on beer infringed the trademark on Black & White whiskey.[62] Use of similar brand names on noncompeting goods can cause confusion, especially as to affiliation, connection, or sponsorship. For example, use of the brand name Yale on flashlights infringed the trademark on Yale locks.[63] Of course, the closer the goods, the more likely the confusion. Put differently: the closer the goods, the less close the other factors need be for confusion to be likely.

## Conditions of Purchase for Goods and Services

The conditions under which purchases are made refer to the care taken and level of understanding consumers have in purchasing goods and services. Obviously, unsophisticated buyers of inexpensive goods are less likely to take care and are more likely confused than sophisticated buyers of expensive goods. For example, an engineer buying expensive electrical testing equipment[64] is less likely to be confused than a child buying candy.[65]

## Other Evidence

Courts find objective evidence reflecting on the likelihood of confusion quite persuasive. While evidence of actual confusion is not required, such evidence is obviously persuasive.[66] Therefore, misdirected letters from confused consumers are the smoking guns of trademark litigation.[67] While in the past the usefulness of survey evidence was not clear, survey evidence showing confusion is now accepted, with the debate focusing on the type and validity of the survey methods. In fact, costly survey evidence — while not technically required — has become a practical require-ment to persuade some judges as to the existence of a likelihood of confusion.[68] Finally, if the brand owner is fortunate enough to find actual evidence the competi-tor intended to confuse consumers, courts readily accept the success of those efforts and find a likelihood of confusion.[69]

## Determining the Strength of the Brand Name

While the five factors discussed above are important in stopping offending uses of similar brand names, the strength of these factors largely depends on the actions of the competitor. The strength of the brand name, however, is something controlled almost entirely by the brand owner when initial branding decisions are made. In choosing a name for a product, it is important to remember that not all brand names are created equal. Courts place words associated with products in one of several cat-egories: generic, descriptive, suggestive, arbitrary, or coined.[70] The category of word is important for several reasons.

### Word Categories

Whether a word is even capable of acting as a trademark depends on into which cat-egory it falls. Coined words (for example, Kodak,[71] Exxon,[72] and Xerox), arbitrary words (for example, Camel,[73] Ivory,[74] and Apple), and suggestive words (for exam-ple, Playboy[75] and Coppertone[76]) are capable of acting as trademarks from the start. Generic words (for example, aspirin,[77] escalator,[78] and cellophane[79]) cannot function as trademarks. More problematic are descriptive words (for example, Chapstick[80] and Tender Vittles[81]) which are capable of trademark status only if an appreciable number of consumers have grown to associate the word with the goods. This asso-ciation is referred to as "secondary meaning." For most purposes, surnames and geo-graphical names are considered descriptive.

The importance of the word category does not end with whether the word is capable of achieving trademark status. The strength of that trademark determines how close a competitor can come to the brand name and goods before a court will step in.[82] The strength of brand name is determined by the impression the name leaves in the minds of consumers. Of course, consumers do not consciously con-sider the scope of a brand name. Thus, the relevant inquiry is what rights consumers subconsciously associate with the brand name. Because of the difficulty in deter-mining the mental state of consumers, again courts look to several factors, includ-ing word category.

In determining the strength of a brand name, coined and arbitrary words are the strongest and descriptive words the weakest. An additional factor is other uses of similar brand names. When choosing a name similar to existing brand names, even on unrelated goods, the brand name weakens. Even if a strong brand name is chosen, allowing use by others of similar names on related goods weakens the brand name. This is an area in which entrepreneurial managers must police others' uses of similar marks.

This categorization scheme has resulted perhaps more in confusion than clarification among those responsible for choosing brand names. The standards used to characterize suggestive marks ("requires imagination, thought, and perception to reach a conclusion about the nature of the goods"[83]) and descriptive marks ("forthwith conveys an immediate idea of the ingredients, qualities or characteristics of the goods"[84]) appear distinct enough. However, when applied to a particular word, this key distinction often defies analysis. This confusion is an unavoidable consequence of drawing hard lines to separate words whose meanings are close on the continuum.

It is helpful to envision a continuum from generic words that are not capable of trademark status to coined words entitled to broad protection. Entrepreneurial managers recognize that implications beyond advertising expenditures depend on where their brand names fall on this continuum. Choosing a word that somehow suggests or describes the goods may be helpful in initially selling a new product; however, the trademark office may refuse to register the word.

For descriptive terms, a period of time passes before secondary meaning is established. During this time, the brand name is particularly vulnerable to imitation. Even if secondary meaning is established, competitors may be able to use uncomfortably close imitations of the brand name or to use the term in its descriptive sense. Thus, entrepreneurial managers weigh the marketing benefit of choosing a highly suggestive or descriptive word against the legal downsides.

Simply choosing a coined or arbitrary word also carries implications for the brand owner. Large marketing expenditures may be required to build consumer awareness in these words. While generally entitled to broader protection, coined words must be policed with vigor; coined words applied to unique products carry a danger that consumers will grow to associate them as the generic identity of the products. For example, the generic terms used as examples above — aspirin, escalator, and cellophane — were all valid trademarks that became generic. Thus, the generic use of brand names is another misuse against which the brand owner must guard. (See Legal Focus: Brand Names Facing Genericide, below.)

When faced with a branding decision, what should entrepreneurial managers do? As a starting point for branding decisions, entrepreneurial managers should consider the same factors on which judges rely. That is, they should examine: whether they or their competitors sell lines of related goods or whether each product exists in its own narrow market; the level of expenditure of customers in buying the goods; and the level of sophistication of the customers. Of course, if these questions are answered differently for different products or product lines, it is important to allow flexibility for different strategies on a division, strategic business unit, product line, or even an individual product level. For example, why expend the resources to originate, develop, and defend a catchy coined brand name for the marketer of expensive electronic laboratory equipment to engineers? This is questionable both in view of the purchasing motivation of the consumers and in light of the high standard a judge would apply in analyzing whether a likelihood of confusion exists. At the opposite end of the spectrum, why not originate, develop, and defend a catchy coined brand name for a new candy product? Again, this is supported both in view of purchaser motivation and in light of a judge's finding of likely confusion between similar brand names.

In addition, entrepreneurial managers should recognize and plan for the inherent conflict between the resource expenditures required to development secondary meaning in highly suggestive (that is, bordering on descriptive) brand names and the most commonly cited reason for adopting highly suggestive brand names — a lack of available resources to develop consumer recognition in the name. Unfortunately, if a highly suggestive name is chosen because the company lacks the resources to develop consumer identification, if secondary meaning develops at all it will take a long period of time during which the brand name is vulnerable. Competitors may be free to use or at least come uncomfortably close to the brand name. Thus, suggestive names should only be used by companies that have the resources to quickly develop consumer recognition.

Acquiring secondary meaning in a highly suggestive word also requires corporate discipline. Brand names should be used only as an adjective to describe a generic name, should never be used as a noun, and should never be used as a verb. Nothing delights an accused competitor more than finding misuses of a brand name by the brand name owner. While some companies are sufficiently disciplined and willing to expend resources to ensure proper internal use, many managers find the temptation to misuse highly suggestive brand names too compelling to resist.

Therefore, using a highly suggestive name requires marketing resources and corporate discipline. But if sufficient resources are available, why not dedicate them to developing an arbitrary or coined name? If resources are not available to develop consumer recognition in an arbitrary or coined name, why not achieve synthesis by developing a distinctive name across more than one product? This can be across a product line, a division, or the entire company. Additionally, why not simply designate individual products within the product line by a generic name, a numerical designation, or even a descriptive name? Examples include Kellogg's Corn Flakes (trade name/trademark plus descriptive name) and Infinity Q45 (trade name/trademark plus numerical designation).

Alternatively, why not use a family of marks that share a common feature to play on previously established consumer recognition?

Examples from McDonald's Corporation:

- McDonald's
- Egg McMuffin
- McChicken
- Chicken McNuggets
- McRib
- Big Mac
- McB.L.T.[85] (See Case Study: Imitation As the Worst Form of Flattery, below.)

Another neglected aspect of branding is choosing a generic name. While this is not typically a factor in mature product markets, when a new product in an infant product market is named an appropriate generic name should also be used. This helps manage the risk of a brand name becoming the generic identifier of a class of products. Thus, if a unique product is introduced, it always should be clearly identified with the generic name, such as Rollerblade brand in-line skates.

Understanding and focusing on the legal implications of branding can lead to better branding decisions. Entrepreneurial managers focus on two primary areas: the legal scope of the term to be used as a brand name, which will determine the strength of the trademark throughout the product life cycle; and a realistic branding strategy that recognizes the available marketing resources and cultural corporate discipline.

## Apple Computer

In introducing the personal computer in 1976, the marketing task was formidable. Prior to the personal computer, computers were large, room-sized equipment that required specially trained operators and special facilities to handle the heat generated by these machines. In order for the personal computer to be successful, a sizable number of consumers had to be convinced computers belonged on their desks. The introducers of the first commercially viable personal computer hit upon an almost perfect branding strategy.

When Stephen "Woz" Wozniak and Steven Jobs founded Apple Computer, their first two models were called Apple I and II. The now famous multi-colored apple logo was based on the slogan of an advertisement for the Apple I circuit boards at the Byte Shops, a nearby computer supply store. Their slogan: Byte into an Apple. Then Apple introduced the Macintosh, a clever play on the name Apple. This wildly successful personal computer began the trend of a personal computer on nearly every desk and in nearly every home.

The choice of Apple as both the trade name and the brand name was brilliant. What image evoked simplicity, friendliness, and commonality better than an apple? What could have been a better connotation for this new personal computer? From a trademark perspective, the choice of Apple also was brilliant. Because apples obviously have no correlation to computers, Apple and Macintosh were arbitrary terms entitled to broad legal protection. This was demonstrated in 1982 when a knock-off computer appeared.

CASE
STUDY

In 1982, Formula International Inc., a small electronics supply store, began selling a computer kit. When assembled, the components in the kit made a personal computer. Formula dubbed their computer kit the Pineapple. Apple took exception. As an arbitrary term entitled to broad legal protection, Apple had little trouble convincing a judge to stop Formula from using the term Pineapple. While a formidable task, choosing a brand name that both sells the product and can be legally protected is possible.

---

CASE

STUDY

## Protectable Trade Decor?

Just how far can the protection of trade dress go? A case decided as much on the audacity of the infringer as on the law shows the outer reaches of the law.

After successfully running several restaurants in Florida, in 1976 Phil Romano moved to San Antonio, Texas to escape Florida's then stagnant economy. He soon concocted a concept for an upscale alternative to fast food. He called his restaurant Fuddruckers, which first opened in San Antonio in 1979 selling fare such as hamburgers, hot dogs, and French fries. Explosive growth was fueled in part by the firm's suggestive advertising, including the tag line: "Get Fresh at Fuddruckers;" a young women exclaiming, "You won't believe how big it is!"; and two men commenting, "Look at those buns!" By 1988, when Unique Casual Restaurants bought out Romano's portion of the stock for $13 million, more than 115 Fuddruckers outlets existed across the United States.

A key to Fuddruckers' concept was the visibility of traditional back-room food preparation. Customers saw employees bake the buns, cut the meat, and cook the food. Food items were stored in bulk in plain view of the customers. Customers "built their own burgers" by adding condiments such as cheese, onions, lettuce, and tomatoes out of large, industrial containers.

The decor of Fuddruckers supported the theme of visibility and utility. Neon signs marked the different areas of the restaurants, mirrors adorned the walls, brown and white tablecloths and flooring adorned the sitting areas, customers sat on brown director's chairs, and yellow awnings marked the restaurant exterior. Two-by-four white tiles were found on the walls, the bar, and the counters. The bakery area was called "Mother Fuddruckers." A restaurant "newspaper" was offered for PR purposes. Customers were allowed to buy bones for their dogs. Large black crock-pots dispensed condiments and a large, plastic garbage pail dispensed ice tea.

In early 1983, Gerald and Doug Koppes became interested in opening a Fuddruckers franchise in Phoenix, Arizona. Unfortunately for the Koppes, a different franchisee was granted rights to Arizona, and plans were announced to open a Fuddruckers in Phoenix. Failing to secure their franchise, the Koppes planned their own restaurant in Phoenix. Their actions left little doubt of their strategy. The Koppes told their bank the closest thing to their new restaurant would be Fuddruckers, sent their designers to Fuddruckers, and described their restaurant in their business plan as very much like Fuddruckers.

Shortly before the franchised Fuddruckers opened in Phoenix, the Koppes opened a restaurant, Doc's B.R.Others, near Phoenix in early December 1983. Doc's B.R.Others' food preparation areas were exposed, neon signs marked the different areas of the restaurant, mirrors adorned the walls, customers sat in director's chairs, and black and white flooring adorned the sitting areas.

The bakery area was called "Mother Others." A restaurant "newspaper" was offered to customers for public relations purposes. Customers were allowed to buy bones for their dogs. The same brand of two-by-four white tiles was on the walls, the bar, and the counters. Large black crock-pots dispensed condiments and even a large, plastic garbage pail dispensed ice tea.

In the inevitable litigation, Doc's B.R.Others won before the trial court and Fuddruckers appealed. The appeals court disagreed with the trial court, concluding this form of flattery went too far. Particularly persuasive was evidence that Fuddruckers received 100 inquiries a week from customers asking if the two restaurants were related. This evidence of actual confusion and the Koppes' strategy obviously went a long way towards showing a likelihood of confusion. Before a second trial could be held, Doc's B.R.Others announced it was bankrupt, and the case was dropped.

CASE
STUDY

CONT.

## Imitation As the Worst Form of Flattery

The persuasiveness of intent in trade dress cases cannot be overstated. In September 1987, Quality Inns International announced a new chain of budget motels to be called "McSleep Inns." This was the result of Quality International's Chief Executive Officer's vision. After becoming CEO in 1980, Robert C. Hazard implemented a marketing strategy that segmented the lodging market into five niches. Clarion Hotels and Resorts targeted the luxury niche, Comfort Inns targeted the luxury-budget niche, and Quality Inns targeted the middle-price niche — he did not target the superluxury niche. Quality International designed a logo consisting of a square shape with rounded corners and a stylized sun that was used with the Clarion Hotels, Comfort Inns, and Quality Inns.

This left the economy niche. In December 1986, Hazard thought he had filled it, when at two o'clock in the morning he thought up the name "McSleep." Denying that the name was tied in any way to McDonald's Corporation, Hazard testified that the "Mc" from the Scottish surname conveyed "thrift."[86]

CASE
STUDY

When the McSleep Inns were scheduled to open in the late eighties, McDonald's had more than 10,000 restaurants in 45 countries and more than $14 billion in annual sales. The legendary Ray Kroc started McDonald's in April 1955 with the opening of its first restaurant in Des Plaines, Illinois, a suburb of Chicago. Over the years that followed, McDonald's sold food products under various brand names, including Egg McMuffin, McChicken, Big Mac, Chicken McNuggets, McRib, McD.L.T., Sausage McMuffin, McFortune Cookie, and McPizza.

While mass marketing its food products primarily to youth, McDonald's promoted its Q.S.C.V. philosophy of Quality, Service, Cleanliness, and Value. In 1966, McDonald's introduced Ronald McDonald, a fictitious clown who presides over McDonaldland. In 1977, McDonald's advertised a fanciful language that featured the formulation of words by combining the "Mc" prefix with nouns and adjectives, such as McService, McPrice, and McBest.

Hazard clearly respected McDonald's. In 1983, he identified nine corporations whose values should be emulated — one was McDonald's. The values he attributed to McDonald's included quality, cleanliness, and value. In 1986, Quality International actually discussed the concept of "McStop," a traveler's plaza including a McDonald's Restaurant, a convenience store, a gas station, and a motel. These discussions broke off in the spring of 1987. Shortly afterward, Hazard instructed his attorneys to register the name McSleep, as well as "McSuite" and "McBudget," at the U.S. Trademark Office.

In presenting his idea of McSleep Inns to his Board of Directors, Hazard openly evoked the McDonald's name, saying "like McDonald's [McSleep] is acceptable for the upscale traveler who wants only a good night's sleep and for the economy traveler who wants to save money." Hazard boasted "the name McSleep should help consumers instantly identify the product." In a publicity article planted with the Washington Post, Hazard was quoted as saying, "Obviously, [the name McSleep is] a takeoff on McDonald's service and quality at a consistent price …. We think we're going to let McDonald's continue to use their name."[87]

Just three days after Quality International's announcement of McSleep, McDonald's demanded they change the name. A lawsuit followed. The court found Hazard's denial of intent unconvincing in light of all his references to McDonald's. The court was not dissuaded by the dissimilarity of the brand names, the difference in the services, and the dissimilar conditions under which the services were purchased. Despite the weakness of these classic factors, the court had little problem finding a conflict based on the strength of the brand name and the evidence of deliberate copying.

Hazard proceeded to introduce his budget motel, now called "Sleep Inn" by dropping the "Mc" prefix, a name change costing just $10,000 given the timing of the motel chain's introduction. McDonald's policing of its "Mc" family of brand names goes on as well. In 1991, McDonald's stopped McPretzel; in 1990, it stopped McTeddy (bears); in 1993, it stopped McDental; and in 1995, it stopped McClaim (legal services).

———⊳◦⊲———

## Brand Names Facing Genericide

Like aspirin, escalator, and cellophane before them, several current brand names have become so ingrained in the consuming public's subconscious that they face so-called "genericide." Current brand names at risk of genericide include Rollerblade, Kleenex, Jeep, Band-Aid, and Post-It. However, by learning valuable lessons from their predecessors, the owners of these brand names are taking action to see that their valuable assets remain alive.

**Legal Focus**

For example, Xerox Corporation spends more than $100,000 a year in advertisements reminding the public of the proper use of its brand — using its brand only as an adjective to describe a generic name (Xerox copier), never using its brand as a noun (instead of copy or copier), and never using its brand as a verb (instead of to copy).[88] One of Xerox's more creative themes took the form of a cartoon cemetery drawn by the late Charles Addams. Under the headline, "Once a Trademark, not always a Trademark," Addam's cartoon showed gravestones with the names of once protectable but now generic terms such as thermos, linoleum, yo-yo, shredded wheat, cube steak, dry ice, nylon, and trampoline. The copy under the ad asked readers to help the company protect the Xerox trademark by using the term correctly.

In defending against genericide, other steps short of litigation can be used. For example, after acquiring the Jeep line of vehicles from American Motors Corporation, Chrysler borrowed a strategy long used in the pharmaceutical industry by designating a generic term for the product category, Sport Utility Vehicle or SUV. Band-Aid not only did likewise, but also defended its trademark by utilizing the tag line, "Band-Aid brand adhesive strip."

## Endnotes

1. Philip Kotler, *Marketing Management*, 6th ed. (Scarborough, Ontario: Prentice-Hall Canada, 1989), 468.

2. J. Thomas McCarthy, *Trademarks and Unfair Competition*, (St. Paul, Minnesota: West Publishing Group, 1996) §4:4H, 129; Jerome Gilson, *Trademark Protection and Practice*, (New York: Matthew Bender, 1990) §1.02[1], 1–13.

3. Kotler, 463.

4. *Trademarks*, Title 15, U.S. CODE, §1127.

5. Ibid.

6. Ibid.

7. *In re McDonald's Corp.*, 230 U.S.P.Q. 210 (Trademark Trials and Appeals Board [T.T.A.B.]), *reversed without published opinion* (Fed. Cir. 1986).

8. *Trademarks*, Title 15, §1127.

9. *Underwriters Laboratories, Inc. v. United Laboratories, Inc.*, 203 U.S.P.Q. 180 (N.D. Ill. 1978).

10. *Trademarks*, Title 17, §1127.

11. *Professional Golfers Association of America v. Bankers Life & Casualty Co.*, 514 F. 2d 665 (5th Cir. 1975).

12. *Trademarks*, Title 15, §1125.

13. Ibid.

14. Gilson, §1.04.

15. *Trademarks*, Title 15, §1125c, 1127; McCarthy, §§24:13–24:16.

16. *Trademarks*, Title 15, §1125c, 127; Gilson, §7.02[6].

17. Gilson, §7.02[6].

18. *Häagen-Dazs, Inc. v. Frusen Glädjé Ltd. A.B.*, 210 U.S.P.Q. 204 (S.D.N.Y. 1980).

19. Ibid.

20. Ibid.

21. *Northern Pacific Railroad Co. v. United States*, 356 U.S. 1 (1958).

22. McCarthy, §3:5.

23. Ibid., §2:7.

24. Ibid., §3:2.

25. Ibid., §3:3.

26. Ibid., §3:4.

27. *James Burrough, Ltd. v. Sign of Beefeater, Inc.*, 540 F. 2d 266 (7th Cir. 1976); *Dallas Cowboys Cheerleaders, Inc. v. Pussycat Cinema, Ltd.*, 604 F. 2d 200 (2d Cir. 1979).

28. Ibid.

29. *Pepsico, Inc. v. The Grapette Co., Inc.*, 416 F. 2d 285 (8th Cir. 1969).

30. *Dawn Donut Co. v. Hart's Food Stores, Inc.*, 267 F. 2d 358 (2d Cir. 1959).

31. *Volkswagenwerk Aktiengesellschaft v. Church*, 411 F. 2d 350 (9th Cir. 1969).

32. *Chanel, Inc. v. Suttner*, 109 U.S.P.Q. 493 (S.D.N.Y. 1956).

33. *Roux Laboratories, Inc. v. Clairol, Inc.*, 427 F. 2d 823 (C.C.P.A. 1970).

34. *Harley-Davidson Motor Co. v. Pierce Foods Corp.*, 231 U.S.P.Q. 857 (T.T.A.B. 1986).

35. *Volkswagenwerk A.G. v. Rickard*, 175 U.S.P.Q. 563 (N.D. Tex. 1972), *modified*, 492 F. 2d 474 (5th Cir. 1984).

36. *Levi Strauss & Co. v. Blue Bell, Inc.*, 200 U.S.P.Q. 434 (C.D. Cal. 1978), *affirmed*, 632 F. 2d 817 (9th Cir. 1980).

37. *Lois Sportswear, U.S.A., Inc. v. Levi Strauss & Co.*, 631 F. Supp. 735 (S.D.N.Y. 1985), *affirmed*, 799 F. 2d 867 (2d Cir. 1986).

38. *In re Dassler*, 134 U.S.P.Q. 265 (T.T.A.B. 1962).

39. *Dallas Cowboys Cheerleaders v. Pussycat Cinema.*

40. *Source Perrier, S.A. v. Waters of Saratoga Springs, Inc.*, 217 U.S.P.Q. 617 (S.D.N.Y. 1982).

41. U.S. Trademark Registration No. 696,147.

42. *In re Weber-Stephen Products Co.*, 3 U.S.P.Q. 2d 1959 (T.T.A.B. 1987).

43. *Rolls-Royce Motors, Ltd. v. A & A Fiberglass, Inc.*, 428 F. Supp. 689 (N.D. Ga. 1977).

44. U.S. Trademark Registration No. 764,837.

45. *Fotomat Corp. v. Cochran*, 437 F. Supp. 1231 (D. Kan. 1977).

46. *Yellow Cab Co. v. Ensler*, 214 Ill. App. 607 (1919); *American Yellow Taxi Operators v. Quinn*, 194 N.Y.S. 623 (1922); *American Yellow Taxi Operators v. Diamond*, 195 N.Y.S. 140 (1922); *Yellow Cab Co. v. Creasman*, 185 N.C. 551 (1923); *Yellow Cab Corp. v. Korpeck*, 198 N.Y.S. 864 (1923); *Yellow Cab Transit Co. v. Louisville Taxicab & Transfer Co.*, 147 F. 2d 407 (6th Cir. 1945).

47. *In re Owens-Corning Fiberglass Corp.*, 774 F. 2d 1116 (Fed. Cir. 1985); *Qualitex Co. v. Jacobson Products Co., Inc.*, 115 S. Ct. 1300 (1995).

48. U.S. Trademark Registration No. 916,533.

49. Gilson, §7.02[7].

50. *Trademarks*, Title 15, §1114.

51. *Grotrain, Helfferich, Schulz, Th. Steinweg Nachf. v. Steinway & Sons*, 365 F. Supp. 707 (S.D.N.Y. 1973), *modified*, 523 F. 2d 1331 (2d Cir. 1975).

52. *McLean v. Fleming*, 96 U.S. 245 (1878).

53. *Polaroid Corp. v. Polarad Electronics Corp.*, 287 F. 2d 492, 495 (2d Cir. 1961).

54. Gilson, §7.02[6].

55. *Esso, Inc. v. Standard Oil Co.*, 98 F. 2d 1 (8th Cir. 1938).

56. *G.D. Searle & Co. v. Chas. Pfizer & Co.*, 265 F. 2d 385 (7th Cir.), *cert. denied*, 361 U.S. 819 (1959).

57. *Coca-Cola Co. v. Clay*, 324 F. 2d 198 (C.C.P.A. 1963).

58. *Cooper's Inc. v. Rocky Mountain Textile, Inc.*, 180 F. Supp. 230 (D. Col. 1959).

59. *S.C. Johnson & Son, Inc. v. Drop Dead Co.*, 210 F. Supp. 816 (S.D. Cal. 1962), *affirmed*, 326 F. 2d 87 (9th Cir. 1963), *cert. denied*, 377 U.S. 907 (1964).

60. *H. Sichel Sohne, GmbH v. Michel Monzain Selected Wines, Inc.*, 202 U.S.P.Q. 62 (T.T.A.B. 1979).

61. *Ex parte Odol-Werke Wien Gesellschaft M.B.H.*, 111 U.S.P.Q. 286 (Comr. Pats. 1956).

62. *Fleischmann Distilling Corp. v. Maier Brewing Co.*, 314 F. 2d 149 (9th Cir.), *cert. denied*, 374 U.S. 830 (1963).

63. *Yale Electric Corp. v. Robertson*, 26 F. 2d 972 (2d Cir. 1928).

64. *Magnaflux Corp. v. Sonoflux Corp.*, 231 F. 2d 669 (C.C.P.A. 1956).

65. *General Foods Corp. v. Mellis*, 203 U.S.P.Q. 261 (S.D.N.Y. 1979).

66. *Tisch Hotels, Inc. v. Americana, Inc.*, 350 F. 2d 609 (7th Cir. 1965).

67. *International Kennel Club, Inc. v. Mighty Star, Inc.*, 846 F. 2d 1079 (7th Cir. 1988).

68. *Mushroom Makers, Inc. v. R.G. Barry Corp.*, 441 F. Supp. 1220 (S.D.N.Y. 1977), *affirmed*, 580 F. 2d 44 (2d Cir. 1978), *cert. denied*, 439 U.S. 1116 (1979); *Mattel, Inc. v. Azrak-Hamway International, Inc.*, 724 F. 2d 357 (2d Cir. 1983); *Universal City Studios, Inc. v. Nintendo Co.*, 746 F. 2d 112 (2d Cir. 1984); *Egal Snacks, Inc. v. Nabisco Brands, Inc.*, 625 F. Supp. 571 (D.N.J. 1985).

69. *My-T-Fine Corp. v. Samuels*, 69 F. 2d 76 (2d Cir. 1934).

70. *Abercrombie & Fitch Co. v. Hunting World, Inc.*, 537 F. 2d 4 (2d Cir. 1976).

71. *Eastman Kodak Co. v. Weil*, 243 N.Y.S. 319 (1930).

72. *Exxon Corp. v. Xoil Energy Resources, Inc.*, 552 F. Supp. 1008 (S.D.N.Y. 1981).

73. *American Association for the Advancement of Science v. The Hearst Corp.*, 206 U.S.P.Q. 605 (D.D.C. 1980).

74. *Abercrombie & Fitch v. Hunting World.*

75. *Playboy Enterprises, Inc. v. Chuckleberry Publishing, Inc.*, 486 F. Supp. 414 (S.D.N.Y. 1980), *affirmed*, 687 F. 2d 563 (2d Cir. 1982).

76. *Douglas Laboratories Corp. v. Cooper Tan, Inc.*, 210 F. 2d 453 (2d Cir.), *cert. denied*, 347 U.S. 968 (1954).

77. *Bayer Co. v. United Drug Co.*, 272 F. 505 (D.N.Y. 1921).

78. *Haughton Elevator Co. v. Seeberger*, 85 U.S.P.Q. 80 (Comr. Pats. 1950).

79. *DuPont Cellophane Co. v. Waxed Products Co.*, 85 F. 2d 75 (2d Cir.), *cert. denied*, 299 U.S. 601 (1986) and 304 U.S. 575, *rehearing denied*, 305 U.S. 672 (1938).

80. *Morton Manufacturing Corp. v. Delland Corp.*, 166 F. 2d 191 (C.C.P.A. 1948).

81. *Ralston Purina Co. v. Thomas J. Lipton, Inc.*, 341 F. Supp. 129 (S.D.N.Y. 1972).

82. *Mobil Oil Corp. v. Pegasus Petroleum Corp.*, 818 F. 2d 254 (2d Cir. 1987).

83. *Stix Products, Inc. v. United Merchants & Manufacturers, Inc.*, 295 F. Supp. 479 (S.D.N.Y. 1968).

84. Ibid.

85. *McDonald's Corp. v. McBagel's Inc.*, 649 F. Supp. 1268 (S.D.N.Y 1986).

86. *Quality Inns International v. McDonald's Corp.*, 8 U.S.P.Q 2d 1633, 1636 (D. Md 1988).

87. Ibid.

88. Steven A. Meyerowitz, "Don't Xerox This Article! How to Defend Your Trademarks," *Business Marketing*, (vol. 69, no. 12) Dec 1984.

## CHAPTER 4

# COPYRIGHTS

**Copyright Due Diligence**

Because the gargle-blaster speaker uses sophisticated digital compression software, George knew his product included valuable embedded software code. While George wrote some of the code, Chip Norton, George's technical wizard, wrote most of it. However, some of the software code used in the gargle-blaster system was in the public domain, while a consultant friend of Chip's also helped him write some of the code. George wasn't sure how the use of an outside consultant could affect his ownership of the software code. Did Marvin Enterprises own the code? Could the consultant sell the code to a competitor? Could the consultant preclude Marvin Enterprises from using that portion of the code the consultant wrote? George suspected that before getting institutional funding, he would need to clear up the ownership of the code.

Like new product technical due diligence, copyright due diligence entails three stages.

- ▶ Does title to the copyright clearly reside with the company?
- ▶ Does exploitation of the copyright infringe on any third party rights?
- ▶ What is the potential value of the copyright?

Based on the nature of the material, none, any, or all of these stages is appropriate.

Even prior to stage one due diligence, steps should have been taken to ensure title to the copyright resides in the company. The rules of creation and ownership of copyrights create special, often overlooked issues of ownership. Anyone involved in creating a copyrighted work should be under a written obligation that ensures the copyrights reside in the company.

While the law provides for employer ownership of works created as part of an employee's job, employment agreements should be in place so no misunderstandings arise about the ownership of works by employees. If consultants were used, they must be under a written obligation that ensures the copyrights reside in the company. If the consultant uses employees or subcontractors, their agreements should be reviewed to ensure that the consultant owns copyrights in the works, so that the consultant has clear title to assign to the company. If rights to the technology are accessed by license, any limitations to the rights licensed — such as a limited field of use — and the financial impact of any royalties as an additional cost-of-goods sold should be considered.

If the copyrighted work is software, all these issues and more should be explored. If software is distributed, care must be taken to ensure these transactions are governed by a written agreement. Due to the unique aspects of copyrights — still the primary source of protection for software — the legal form of this type of transaction must be a license. Failure to document this license may result in loss of significant intellectual property rights.

In stage two due diligence, focus is on whether exploitation of the copyright could infringe on third party rights. Because infringement of a copyright involves access to the copyrighted work, care must be taken that any copyrighted works were derived independently from prior copyrights. For example, a second author who refines a first author's copyrighted work can copyright the derivative work separately from the original work. However, because the second author had access and the derivative work is substantially similar to the original work, the second author cannot exploit the derivative work without infringing the copyright of the first author. In this circumstance, care must be taken to ensure the first work is licensed.

In stage three due diligence, the potential value of the intellectual property should be understood so the level of competition from economic substitute products can be considered. For example, if a software product is not protected by a patent, but is copyrighted, pricing strategies and marketplace penetration should take into account the likelihood of competition from substitute products. This is because a patent is the only form of intellectual property that can prevent duplication of the basic functionality of a product. The copyright does not protect the idea embodied in a product, only the expression of that idea. Thus, a strategy focused on quickly building brand equity to further protect the product should be considered.

Taking the ownership bull by the horns, George talked to Chip about the code Chip's friend had written. George was pleased to find out that Chip's friend had been

**Stage One Due Diligence**

**Stage Two Due Diligence**

**Stage Three Due Diligence**

paid for the work he performed, but was concerned that Chip hadn't had his friend sign any documentation regarding that work. Chip was certain that his friend had understood that Marvin Industries would "own" the code for which they had paid him. Nevertheless, George let Chip know that they needed to have Chip's friend assign any right he retained over to Marvin Industries. Because Chip planned on using his friend for future Marvin Industries projects, Chip and George hoped that getting a signed assignment wouldn't be a problem.

In addition to clear title, George was concerned with protecting the sophisticated digital compression software used in the gargle-blaster speakers. In talking to Chip, they were concerned that an offshore competitor could reverse engineer the digital compression software and create a package that would retro-fit existing speakers with their technology. While hopefully someday their patents could be used to stop this, that prospect was at least several years away given the delay in issuing a patent. If retro-fit packages were already available, the possibility of stopping this activity when a patent issued was depressingly slim. Once the software was out of the bag, it would be all over the Internet, freely available to all.

George was aware of the lengths software developers went to protect their software products, through written contracts and "shrink-wrap" licensing. Since the gargle-blaster speakers included valuable software, did he need a shrink-wrap license? George wondered what the risk would be for not having a written agreement. George knew he needed to better understand copyrights and how they related to his sale of speakers before deciding these issues.

## Overview of the Copyright Laws

Unlike patents, which protect the technological application of an idea, or trademarks, which protect against the confusion of consumers, copyrights protect against the duplication of an expression of an idea and not the idea itself. Thus, in a classic example, the expression of the tragic death of lovers from rival groups in *West Side Story* would not have infringed on Shakespeare's *Romeo and Juliet*, had Shakespeare owned a copyright. (For a description of the process and costs of filing a copyright, see Appendix C.) Unlike patents, which require the technological application of an idea be a nonobvious advance in technology, copyrights require only originality in the expression of the idea and not novelty in the idea itself. Thus, the author of *West Side Story* was entitled to a copyright on his original expression of the idea of the tragic death of lovers from rival groups, even though Shakespeare — and perhaps many others — previously expressed similar ideas. In further contrast to patents, which include some requirement that the invention be useful, copyrights do not extend to functional objects. Thus, if a functional object is in the class of patentable subject matter — even if it is not sufficiently inventive to be entitled to a patent — copyright protection should be denied.[1] Similarly, business ideas such as accounting systems[2] or marketing concepts[3] are not copyrightable, because they involve ideas, not expression.

Which is not to say that parts of functional objects cannot be copyrighted. Copyrights protect nonfunctional aspects of objects, such as the artistic expression found in the base of a lamp.[4] Likewise, while architectural structures were long considered functional and thus not copyrightable, artistic expression found in an art deco relief or a classical column, for example, could always be copyrighted.[5] To address what many believed to be unfair treatment of architectural designs, Congress passed a law in 1990 to specifically cover building designs under the copyright laws.[6]

The result of the utility/nonutility dichotomy is that, while a wide array of objects are copyrightable, the extent of the copyrightable expression is limited for many objects. Thus, business forms are copyrightable, but the copyright extends only to those aspects of the form that are nonfunctional. A list of data is copyrightable, but the copyright extends only to the format of the listing and not the data itself. Thus, the extent to which a list of data is copyrightable extends on a continuum from the unprotectable data itself, to the maybe protectable selection of which data to include, to the relatively protectable arrangement.[7] Likewise, the extent to which a play is copyrightable extends on a continuum from the unprotectable idea, to the relatively unprotectable theme, to the maybe protectable plot, to the relatively protectable incident, to the clearly protectable dialogue.[8]

Likewise, while a computer program is copyrightable, the copyright extends only to the expression of an idea — most likely the source code, object code, and micro code, not to the idea itself — most likely not the sequence, structure, or organization. Because of the limits of copyright protection on software, software companies have buttressed their protection. Nearly all software licenses contain language that prohibits reverse engineering of the sequence, structure, or organization of the software; for example, "Licensee agrees it will not, and will not authorize any third party to translate, reverse engineer, decompile, disassemble, or make any other unauthorized use of the Licensed Software." While the enforceability of these provisions is not entirely clear (see Legal Focus: Reverse Engineering Software, below), many courts have upheld these provisions.

In the copyright statute, Congress mentioned several categories of copyrightable material:

- books
- computer programs
- computer disks
- films
- fine art
- globes
- graphic art
- maps
- motion pictures
- music
- sculpture
- video disks
- videotapes[9]

Live musical performances are protected under a related but separate law.[10]

Procuring a copyright is extremely affordable. Prior to 1989, a lack of copyright notice could have serious effects on copyright; since 1989 notice has not been required. However, notice achieves the business goal of informing competitors that the work is valuable property that will be defended. It also proves conclusively the date of creation and makes certain damages available. In addition, before bringing suit for copyright infringement, the work must be registered at the copyright office. Thus, a copyright owner can wait to register the work until a need to enforce the copyright exists. Again, registration is valuable to show competitors the seriousness with which owners view their rights, make certain damages available, and conclusively prove the date of creation.

The limits of copyrights are best understood by understanding how to show infringement. To prove infringement of a copyright, the owner must show that the infringer had access to the copyrighted work and the resulting work is substantially similar to the copyrighted work. Once these have been shown, it is up to the accused to show infringement has not occurred, often through lack of access.[11]

Of course, the substantial similarity must be to the appropriate expression of the idea; substantial similarity to the idea itself is not an infringement. Thus, if the accused shows both works are substantially similar to material in the public domain, such as an historical event, they have gone a long way towards showing the copyrightable expression has not been copied.

The Copyright Act itself categorizes the types of copying that are prohibited: reproductions, derivative works, performance, distribution, and display.[12] The prohibition against reproduction simply means a copyrighted work cannot be copied. Derivative works refer to a recast, transformation, or adaptation of a copyrighted work, such as a translation, arrangement, dramatization, fictionalization, film, recording, abridgement, or condensation.

Performance includes the public display of literary, musical, dramatic, choreographic, pantomime, movie, or other audio/visual works. This category does not apply to visual arts, sound recordings, or pictorial, graphic, and sculptural works. The exclusion of sound recordings means that owners of copyrights on the production or performance of music have no ability to prohibit public performances, with that right reserved to composers.

The distribution and display categories actually limit the reach of the copyright after the sale of a copyrighted work. Once a sale of a copyrighted work occurs, the buyer can sell the work to another without violating the copyright laws. The new owner can display the work, but the new owner can neither make copies of the work nor display multiple images of the work, such as, for example, through display on multiple computer screens.

A significant right of authors that has for years been a factor outside the United States is finally making its way into the United States. Moral rights refer to the protection of authors' professional honor and reputation in their works. Moral rights give the author the right of attribution, that is the right to claim or disclaim authorship in the work, and the right of integrity, which is the right to object to the distortion, mutilation or other modification, or other derogatory act to the work.

The rights of authors to attribution and integrity apply even if the copyright to the work is transferred. In 1990, Congress passed an act applying the rights of attribution and integrity to paintings, drawings, prints, sculptures, and limited-distribution, still-photographic images.[13]

The "fair use" defense mitigates the broad prohibition against copying. The fair use defense admits access and substantial similarity, but relies on public policy that some forms of copying are acceptable. Whether an act of copying is a fair use depends on several factors: the commercial versus educational aspects of the copied use; the degree of expression encompassed in the copyrighted work; the amount and importance of the copied use; and the economic impact of the use on the market for the copyrighted work.

## Ownership

Ownership of copyrights involves unique concepts of which an entrepreneurial manager should be aware. There is a distinction between owning the physical object that embodies the copyright, such as a sculpture or original music sheet, and the ownership of the copyright on the expression in the sculpture or music. Without an express written conveyance of the copyright, ownership of the physical object does not convey the underlying copyright.

Additionally, more than one copyright can underlie a single work. For example, an author who compiles stories or essays into an anthology can copyright the collection, but the copyrights of the parts remain with the contributing authors. One author can copyright the lyrics of a song, another author can copyright the music. If the lyricist and the composer worked with the intent of combining the two works, they are joint owners of a united copyright.

In a situation analogous to an improvement patent, a second author who refines a first author's copyrighted work can copyright the derivative work separately from the original work. While the first author can exploit the right to the first copyrighted work without the permission of the second author, the first author cannot exploit the copyrighted derivative work without the permission of the second author. The second author can prevent the first author from using the copyright on the derivative work; however, because the second author had access and the derivative work is substantially similar to the original work, the second author cannot exploit the derivative work without the permission of the first author.

## Work-for-Hire

While authors typically own the copyright upon creation of a work, someone other than the creator can own the copyright of an original work if it is a "work-for-hire." A work-for-hire must fit into one of two categories:

- ▸ Works created by employees within the scope of their employment.
- ▸ Works that are specifically commissioned under a written agreement, provided the work is within one of nine categories: contributions to collective works; parts of motion pictures or audio-visual aids; translations; supplemental works (for example, forewords); compilations; instructional texts; tests; test answers; and atlases.[14]

In addition, an agreement to transfer ownership in a copyright must be in writing, according to law. Because of the uncertainty in copyright ownership, any works created by an independent consultant should be covered by a written agreement and should contain ownership language:

> Each copyrightable work, to the extent permitted by law, will be considered a work-made-for-hire with the authorship and copyright of the work in Company's name. To the extent any such copyrightable work cannot be considered a work-made-for-hire, Consultant agrees to assign to the Company all right, title, and interest in and to the copyrightable work.

According to these rules, if a software program is made entirely by employees of a company hired to write software, the company owns the copyright. If an independent consultant writes the software, the consultant owns the copyright in the absence of a written agreement. If an employee and an independent consultant jointly write software in the absence of a written agreement, the copyright will be held jointly by the company and the consultant. If the employee wrote a software program and an independent consultant was later hired to write an improved version of the software program, the company would own the underlying copyright while the consultant would own the copyright in the derivative work.

If the rules on ownership are complicated, the rules on the term of a copyright are convoluted. Because the term of a copyright is extremely long, ranging from 70 to more than 120 years, the expiration date is largely academic for many works, such as software. The technology becomes obsolete long before the copyright expires.

The term of a copyright can depend on the type of ownership as well as the date of creation. It is generally the life of the owner plus 50 years.[15] If a joint work, the term is the life of the last author to die plus 50 years.[16] If a work was for hire, the term is the earlier of 75 years after publication or 100 years after creation.[17] Because of several changes in the law, the term can also vary depending on when the copyrighted work was created.

In a provision designed to protect authors who transfer their copyrights and later find the value to have been increased, the Act provides that authors who sold their copyrights can recapture their rights 31 years later. This provision does not apply to works-for-hire.

## Clean Room Design

Legal Focus

To avoid infringing a copyright, a so-called "clean room" design process can be used. To prove infringement of a copyright, the copyright owner must show the infringer had access to the copyrighted work and the resulting work is substantially similar to the copyrighted work. The clean room design process is designed to avoid access to the copyrighted work.

In a clean room design, the functional aspects of a copyrighted product are compiled. For example, a software development team decompiles a software program into a functional product/requirements specification. This functional product/requirements specification is provided to a different software development team that has not been exposed to the copyrighted material, so the expression of the idea is not copied in designing a new product. The functional product/requirements specification should not include source code, object code, or micro code. While information regarding the idea of the software can include reference to the sequence, structure, or organization, the boundary of information is probably drawn before the use of flow charts of the software, which some courts have found copyrightable. Legal counsel typically reviews the functional product/requirements specification to ensure no copyrighted information has been included.

Demonstrating that the second development team has not been exposed to the copyrighted material is a matter of factual proof. If the members of the two development teams work in a common area, lunch together or go after work for beers at the local watering hole, a determiner of the facts — either a judge or jury — may have a hard time believing those in the clean room didn't get "dirty." Thus, companies often use outside consultants as one of the development teams.

Software companies have fought back against clean room development by including language in their software licenses that prohibit this activity — for example, "Licensee agrees it will not translate, reverse engineer, decompile, or disassemble the Licensed Software." While the enforceability of these provisions is somewhat unsettled, many courts have held clean room designs breach this type of contract. (See Legal Focus: Reverse Engineering Software, below.) Thus, before embarking on a clean room design, the terms of any license agreement should be reviewed by legal counsel.

## Reverse Engineering Software

Legal Focus

When an attorney says the law is unsettled, consider two cases. On one hand, in 1994, Matthew Zeidenberg, a Ph.D. candidate in computer science at the University

Legal Focus
(continued)

of Wisconsin, bought a copy of ProCD's SelectPhone product from a retail outlet in Madison, Wisconsin. The SelectPhone product was on CD-ROM disks and included data compiled from more than 3,000 telephone directories, containing more than 95 million residential and commercial listings. The listings included full names, street addresses, telephone numbers, zip codes, and industry or SIC codes. The database cost more than $10 million to compile. ProCD sold the database to the general consuming public for $150, but charged industrial customers more. Zeidenberg downloaded the telephone listings from the CD-ROM disks of this product and placed the data onto an Internet host computer to make the listings available — at a price — to Internet users. ProCD sued.

The SelectPhone product was sold with a "shrink-wrap" license. In ProCD's form, the box declared that the software was licensed with restrictions stated in the enclosed contract. The opening paragraph of the contract stated:

> Please read this license carefully before using the software or accessing the listings contained on the disks. By using the disks and the listings licensed to you, you agree to be bound by the terms of this License. If you do not agree to the terms of this License, promptly return all copies of the software, listings that may have been exported, the disks, and the User's Guide to the place where you obtained it .... You will not make the Software or the Listings in whole or in part available to any other user in any networked or timeshared environment, or transfer the listings in whole or in part to any computer other than the computer used to access the Listings.[18]

The contract was encoded on the CD-ROM disks as well as printed in the user's manual. The contract also appeared on a user's screen every time the software was accessed. The court had to decide, did federal copyright law forbid the enforcement of these contracts? The Seventh Circuit Court of Appeals — the Federal Appeals court with jurisdiction over Illinois, Indiana, and Wisconsin — ruled no. Importantly, the court rejected the argument that such shrink-wrap licenses unlawfully extended the copyright laws, which allowed copying of the unprotectable data listings.

In the other case, Vault Corporation produced computer diskettes sold under the Prolok brand. This product was designed to prevent unauthorized duplication of programs placed on the diskettes by software companies, Vault's customers. Vault used a "fingerprint," which is a small mark physically placed on the magnetic surface of each Prolok diskette that contains information that cannot be altered or erased. To operate a computer using a Prolok diskette, the computer must verify the original fingerprint.

Quaide Software Ltd. sold a product in Louisiana called Ramkey, which was specifically designed to unlock the Prolok protection device. The Ramkey product makes it appear to a computer that a copied diskette contains the fingerprint. Vault sued.

In adjudicating the case, the court had to decide whether federal copyright law preempted the enforcement of these contracts. The Fifth Circuit Court of Appeals — the federal appeals court with jurisdiction over Texas, Louisiana, and Mississippi — ruled yes. Importantly, the court accepted the argument that such shrink-wrap licenses unlawfully extended the copyright laws, which allow the reverse engineering of the unprotectable ideas in the program.

These cases clearly contradict each other because of the opposite rulings on the enforceability of shrink-wrap licenses. However, because of the national market for software, no software developer can avoid distribution of their product into those states governed by the Seventh Circuit. Thus, the more restrictive ruling, that shrink-wrap licenses can preclude copying of unprotectable parts of the software, is by default the standard.

## Napster

"... Yeah, I feel like I'm being stolen from, and I'd like to knock that punk around that invented it, but it was bound to happen . . .. I think Metallica's got the right idea: sue 'em. It's your copyright, it is copyright infringement, ..."

— Goo Goo Dolls singer/guitarist Johnny Rzeznik, *Sonicnet.com*, 7 June 2000.

It is undoubtedly not the first time a business has been predicated on a legal loophole. In October 1999, 19-year-old Shawn Fanning formed a company called Napster to exploit his MusicShare software program, written to allow individuals to share music files over the Internet. Napster was backed by San Francisco-based venture capital firm Hummer Winblad. In May 2000, Hummer Winblad led a $15 million round of funding — including $13 million of its own — and installed partner Hank Barry as Napster's acting CEO and name partner John Hummer, once a professional basketball player for the Seattle SuperSonics, as a board director. However, not even rumpled superlawyer David Boies, slayer of the Microsoft antitrust giant and defender of all Floridians' right to vote, could ultimately save the day.

Fanning's MusicShare software can be downloaded from the website in less than a minute. Once the software is configured, the user can begin searching for digital music files that are kept on the hard drives of all the people who have previously downloaded the program. Any songs that you download via Napster can then be retrieved from others via your computer. First, the user enters the music into the Napster search engine. The program then searches other users' computers via the Internet to find the music file. The user then copies and transfers the digital music file from the computer with the file to the user's computer.

Despite what may have seemed like blatant copyright infringement to some, offering free music over the Internet gained users fast. In six months, there were

**Legal Focus**
(continued)

CASE
STUDY

nearly 800,000 files available for download on the Napster website. In a year, Napster registered over 5 million users. In 15 months, Napster accrued 20 million users — a feat that took America Online nearly 15 years to achieve.

It took just two months, until December, for the Recording Industry Association of America (RIAA), which represents the major music labels, to sue the startup. The case took on a higher profile when popular heavy-metal group Metallica joined the fray, asking Napster to bar access to the service by users who had downloaded the band's songs. The RIAA basically argued that the site promotes piracy and copyright infringement. Because Napster itself does not store or transfer files, it cannot be liable for direct infringement. Instead, the RIAA argued that Napster's actions facilitated direct infringement of copyright by its users.

Napster's defense was that its users' conduct amounted to "space-shifting" of a file already stored on a user's hard-drive to a portable listening device, which the court had previously found to be noninfringing.[19] Napster further argued that its users' conduct amounted to "time-shifting," like recording a television program on videotape for later viewing, which the Supreme Court had also found to be noninfringing.[20]

The courts were unmoved. In July, the trial judge ruled in favor of the recording industry and ordered the company to shut down any trading of copyrighted files. In February 2001, the Court of Appeals for the Ninth Circuit affirmed Napster's liability for causing the copyright infringement of its users.

———※———

George talked to his attorney about the value of the digital compression software used in the gargle-blaster speakers and the real threat that an offshore competitor could reverse engineer the digital compression software and create a package that would retro-fit existing speakers with their technology. Even though the gargle-blasters would be relatively expensive audio equipment targeted at the high end of the consumer electronics market, George rejected as impractical his attorney's suggestion that he negotiate and sign each purchaser to an individual contract for each speaker purchase. However, George decided to "shrink-wrap" his speakers in order to create a license to the software so he could better protect its use.

## Endnotes

1. *Bonito Boats, Inc. v. Thunder Craft Boats, Inc.*, 489 U.S. 141 (1989).

2. *Baker v. Selden*, 101 U.S. 99 (1880).

3. *Häagen-Dazs, Inc. v. Frusen Glädjé Ltd. A.B.*, 210 U.S.P.Q. 204 (S.D.N.Y. 1980).

4. *Mazer v. Stein*, 101 U.S. 99 (1954).

5. *Copyright Act*, Public Law 533, 94th Cong., 2d Sess. 63 (1976), H. Rept. 1476.

6. *Copyrights*, Title 17, U.S. CODE, §101.

7. *Feist Publications, Inc. v. Rural Telephone Services Co.*, 99 US 340 (1991).

8. *Sheldon v. Metro Goldwyn Pictures Corp.*, 81 F. 2d 49 (2d Cir., 1936).

9. *Copyrights*, Title 17, §101; *Copyright Act*.

10. *Copyrights*, Title 17, §1101.

11. *Ferguson v. NBC*, 584 F. 2d 111 (5th Cir. 1978).

12. *Copyrights*, Title 17, §106.

13. Ibid., §106a.

14. Ibid., §101.

15. Ibid., §302a.

16. Ibid., §302b.

17. Ibid., §302c.

18. *ProCD, Inc. v. Zeidenberg*. 38 U.S.P.Q 2d 1513, 1515 (W.D. Wis.), *overruled*, 86 F. 3d 1447 (7th Cir. 1996).

19. *Recording Industry Association v. Diamond Multimedia Systems., Inc.*, 180 F. 3d 1072, 1079 (9th Cir. 1999).

20. *Sony Corp. v. Universal City Studios, Inc.*, 464 U.S. 417, 423 (1984).

## CHAPTER 5

# PATENT
# ECONOMICS

Because he had always been interested in becoming an entrepreneur, George took business electives in economics while earning his engineering degree. Thus, he had a good background in economics. Nevertheless, George was confused about the economics of patents. He understood what patents could achieve for him in the marketplace: the ability to exclude substitute products so he could charge a premium price. However, whenever he mentioned the term "monopoly" in the presence of his attorneys, he was immediately scolded. But if a patent didn't give the patent owner an economic monopoly, what good was it?

To make pricing decisions for his gargle-blaster speakers, he needed to understand how his patents would keep the competition at bay. Would he get a 20-year monopoly on selling the speakers? Would he get a couple of years head start before his competitors could get around the patents? Would he face competition from inferior products that claimed to allow the same advantages as his technology? Also, necessarily related to his pricing decision was his strategy on market penetration for the gargle-blaster speakers. Should he try a staged product introduction, first at the high end, then with increasingly less expensive mainstream products? Should he introduce the product to the mainstream first with a large marketing splash to gain market share and establish his brand as the premier speaker technology? In order to make intelligent decisions on these issues, he needed to understand not just the patent laws, but also the economic effects of patents in the marketplace.

## Supply and Demand

In understanding the economics of patents, the place to start is the classic economic marketplace model — the supply and demand curve. With quantity on the horizontal axis and price on the vertical axis, the price and output are set by the intersection of the downwardly sloping demand curve and the upwardly sloping supply curve (see fig. 5-1).

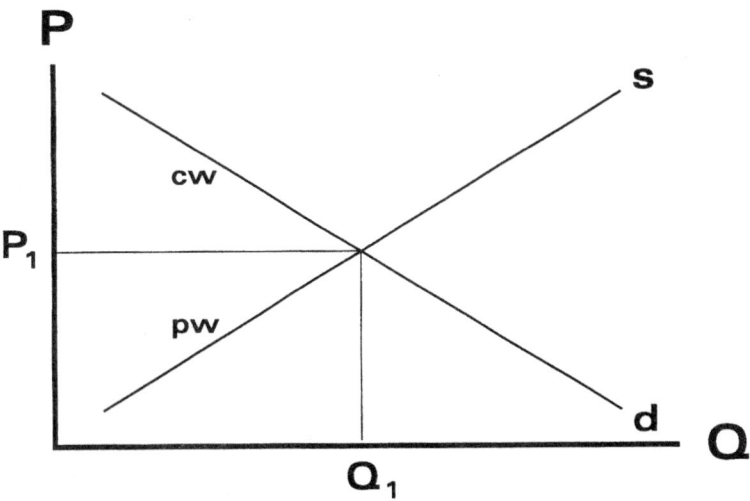

**Fig. 5-1. Perfect Competition Market**

The upwardly sloping supply curve (s) indicates that as the price of goods increases, producers increase output of the goods because products can be made at a profit. The downwardly sloping demand curve (d) indicates that as the quantity of goods available in the market increases, the price decreases because increased competition drives prices down. Equilibrium market price (p) and quantity (q) are determined by the intersection of supply and demand.

In this classical model, the area above the market price and below the demand curve is consumer welfare. This consumer welfare is the gain to consumers willing to pay more than the market price for goods, but who can buy the goods at the lower market price. The area below the market price and above the supply curve is producer welfare. This producer welfare is the gain to producers willing to produce and sell goods at a lower price, but who can sell the goods at the higher market price.

One reason the demand curve slopes downward is substitute goods. If prices increase, a number of consumers will switch to substitute goods. For example, if the price of toasted corn flakes increases, some consumers will buy puffed rice instead of paying the higher price. If the price of toasted corn flakes increases enough, almost all consumers will switch to puffed rice. The degree to which consumers are willing to switch to substitute goods is referred to as "price elasticity of demand." The more willing consumers are to switch — or correspondingly, the closer the substitute goods — the higher the price elasticity of demand.

## Price Elasticity

Price elasticity of demand is an important key to assessing the role of an individual firm in a perfectly competitive market. Within a perfectly competitive market, perfect substitute products exist. Thus, the price elasticity of demand within a perfectly competitive market is infinite. In a perfectly competitive market, if 100 firms produce toasted corn flakes and one firm increases the price, consumers will simply buy the lower-priced corn flakes of one of the other 99 firms. This means an individual firm in a perfectly competitive industry is a price taker. That is, the forces of supply and demand on the market as a whole define the price the firm must accept. At a given market price, the firm will continue producing so long as the marginal cost (the additional cost of producing an additional product) is less than the marginal revenue (the additional revenue received from selling an additional product). In addition, because the market sets the price, the marginal revenue to the firm equals the market price as seen in figure 5-2.

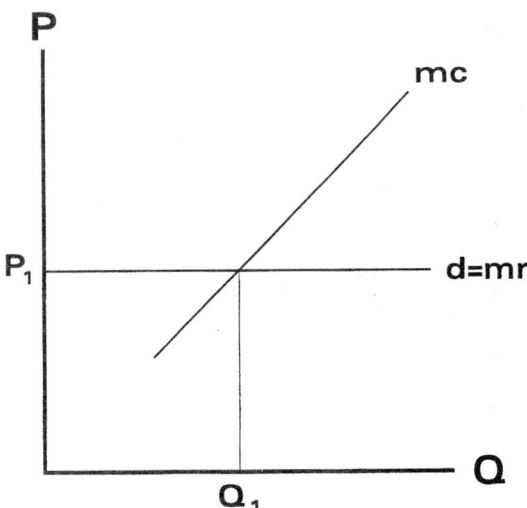

**Fig. 5-2. Perfect Competition Firm**

This makes sense because no firm will produce products when the marginal cost of producing a product exceeds the market price received from selling that product. Thus, a profit-maximizing firm will produce up to that point where marginal revenue equals marginal costs — that is, up to that point where a profit is no longer made by selling an additional product.

## The Patent Profit

A firm with a patented product does not operate in a perfectly competitive market, however. As a reward for innovation, the patent allows the firm to exclude from the market perfect substitute products. Unlike the firm in the perfectly competitive model seen in figure 5-2, a firm producing a patented product has a downwardly sloping demand curve. In other words, the higher the price, the less quantity is sold. The marginal cost of producing a patented product is the same as the marginal cost of producing the product if not patented.

The marginal revenue curve intersects the price axis at the same point as the demand curve, but slopes downwardly at twice the rate as the demand curve, because to sell an additional patented product at a lower price all the patented products must be sold at this lower price. Thus, an individual firm selling a patented product enjoys a protected market, as illustrated in figure 5-3. For the same reasons as before, the firm will sell a quantity where marginal revenue equals marginal costs. At this quantity, the demand curve determines the price. This price (Pp) is greater than the price the product would be if not patented (Pg).

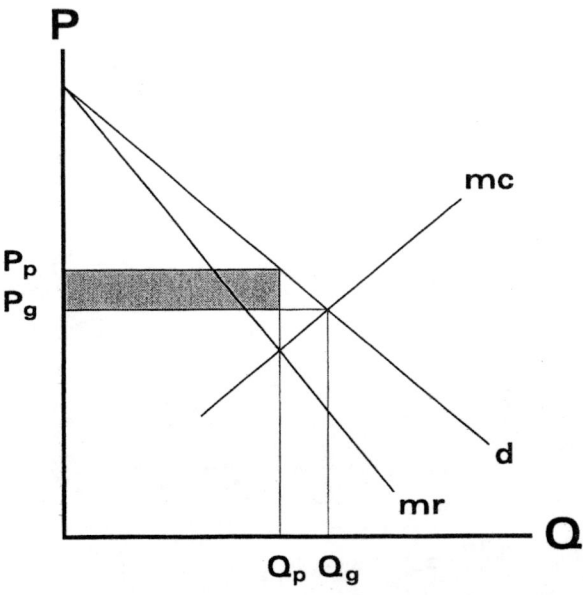

**Fig. 5-3. Protected Competition Firm**

The patent allows the firm to gain an extra profit. If the patent did not exist, competitors could freely copy the product and perfect substitutes would exist. In the absence of the patent, the demand curve and the marginal revenue curve would be horizontal. Also, the quantity produced would increase while the price would fall. The ability to charge a higher price transfers welfare from consumers, who pay the higher price, to the producer, who receives the higher price. This is represented as the difference in area between the higher price the patented product commands and the lower price an unpatented product achieves, set by the intersection of the marginal cost curve and the demand curve. This area represents the special profit — the patent profit — that goes to the producer of a patented product. This higher price also results in deadweight loss to society, represented by the triangle to the right of the patent profit. This area is lost to consumers who cannot afford to pay the higher price but is not gained by the producer because no product is sold to these consumers. Deadweight loss represents the cost to society of a patent system, against which must be measured the benefit to society of increased innovation.

Not all patented products command the same patent profit. The amount of patent profit is defined by how closely noninfringing substitute products can duplicate the patented product. For example, if only one firm can produce toasted corn flakes but many firms produce puffed rice, an increase in the price of toasted corn flakes will cause some consumers to switch to puffed rice. While not a perfect substitute, puffed rice is a substitute product. The willingness of consumers to switch to noninfringing substitutes defines the value of the patent or, in economic terms, the value of the patent profit is defined by the price elasticity of demand. The price elasticity of demand for a patented product is defined by several factors.

Initially, the scope of the patent affects the price elasticity of demand. A broad, pioneer patent has a much greater — although not absolute — potential to decrease the price elasticity of demand than a narrow patent. However, the breadth of the patent is not the sole determinant of price elasticity. The degree to which alternative technologies that do not infringe the patent can perform similarly to the patented technology affects the price elasticity of demand. If a noninfringing substitute technology achieves the same benefits as a patented technology at the same costs, the price elasticity of demand increases. The market demand for the technological improvements will affect the price elasticity of demand. Even if a technologically superior product can be made that a patent broadly protects, if the technological improvement does not meet a market need, the price elasticity of demand is high.

These principles can be seen in two models of patented products in figure 5-4. In the first model, the various factors result in high price elasticity of demand. In the second model, these factors result in a low price elasticity of demand. The difference in patent profit can be seen in the different areas representing the patent profit. The valuation of patents, according to sound financial principles, should be based on this patent profit over any other valuation scheme.

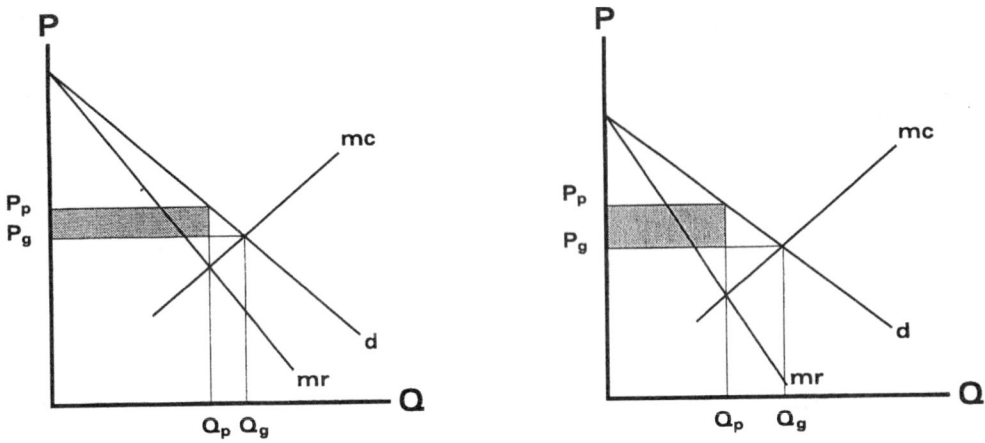

**Fig. 5-4. Two Patented Products**

## Valuing Patents – The Finance of Licensing Patents

Like many startups, George's business plan included well-thought-out product expansion into several areas. While admittedly the chances of hitting a home run in many of the areas was a long shot, George was dismayed at the degree to which the venture capitalists discounted the potential of these markets. While initially determined to make some of these areas pay off, the chance of focusing the time, energy, and resources to penetrate these markets was growing increasingly distant given the challenges of growth. And with the increasing recognition that future product expansion should be directed towards products that complemented his successful product, George was beginning to wonder if the venture capitalists were right.

In the prior sections, the appropriate economic foundation for valuing patents was explored. The appropriate foundation is the patent profit a patent owner receives in the market by virtue of the patent's ability to exclude perfect substitute products. The proper analysis for valuation of this patent profit will be discussed, including an analysis for dividing this patent profit in licensing.

### Inappropriate Valuation

Initially, it is important to expose the inappropriateness of several valuation schemes that are often endorsed but do not directly relate to the patent profit. The first is the so-called "industry norm." Comparable to pricing all houses in a given town at the same price, this analysis seeks to prescribe a standard royalty for patents in a given industry as a method of valuing the patent.

The problem with this method is it does not relate at any level to the degree to which the patent can exclude substitute products and command a patent profit. Not all patents in any given industry bear the same ability to exclude substitutes. When industry norm is used, patents that represent a minor yet profitable ability to exclude substitutes will not be exploited. These patents will not justify payment by any licensee of this industry norm.

Likewise, the opportunity to license and therefore exploit patents that represent a broad ability to exclude substitutes will be lost by companies employing the industry norm. This is because enlightened competitors will outbid them for the license by paying higher royalties supportable by the broad patent. The enlightened competitor can afford to do this because the patent profit on those patents will be greater than the patent profit reflected in the industry norm. The industry norm method of valuation results in exploitation of only a narrow band of patents whose value happens to equal the industry norm. Opportunities outside this narrow band are lost.

A second method prescribes a portion of the total profits that result from commercializing the patented technology as a method of valuing the patent. Comparable to pricing all houses in a given town at the same markup over the construction costs, a typical rule of thumb under this method is for the licensor to command 25 percent of the profit. This method at least links the value of the patent to the profitability of commercial exploitation. However, because it does not relate to the value and degree to which the patent can exclude substitute products and therefore command a patent profit, it is little better than the industry norm.

Despite the inappropriateness of these methods, they retain widespread endorsement and use. Two reasons account for this. First is the simplicity of the analysis. In analyzing whether to license technology, it is much easier to apply a canned formula than to establish the value of unique assets on a case-by-case basis. However, firms that use simplistic business analysis will make poor decisions and lose opportunities.

The second reason for the continued use of these methods is that, for a given business enterprise, use of these methods becomes a self-fulfilling prophecy. If a business development professional is supplied with a canned formula to use in analyzing licensing opportunities, it is straightforward to determine whether the opportunity makes sense. The business development professional will simply pass on those patents that have a value less than this arbitrary formula requires, concluding the opportunity is not profitable.

For those patents having a value that falls into the narrow band defined by the formula, the business development professional will conclude licensing is profitable and, if this rate is acceptable to the licensor, a deal will result. For those patents that have a value above the arbitrary formula, the business development professional will enthusiastically embrace a license. If the firm's competitors are equally unenlightened, and a deal is struck, the business development professional will point to the windfall profit as a further confirmation of the rule of thumb. If the firm has an enlightened competitor that outbids the firm, the business development professional will scoff at the foolishness of the competitor paying more than the industry norm, but will lose the opportunity.

## Appropriate Patent Valuation

Enlightened competitors bid more because they understand and have estimated the patent profit. To appropriately value the patent, the patent profit must be the foundation. This is done by first modeling the sales volume and price for the new product — an estimate to be sure, but a sound business estimate that should be calculated in any new product introduction. This analysis provides an estimate for the volume at which the marginal cost and marginal revenue curves intersect and thus the product price. The price model should include an analysis of the price of the new product, including the price the market will pay for the advantage the patented product represents over substitute products. This is another estimate to be sure, but once again, a sound business estimate that should be calculated in any new product introduction.

The licensor will not license the technology unless a fair portion of this special profit is retained. The licensee will not produce products embodying the technology unless a fair return on the cost and risks of new product introduction is retained. Thus, once the patent profit for each product is determined, it is apportioned between the licensor and the licensee. Market conditions help determine a fair apportionment. Factors such as high risk of commercialization, large capital investments to bring the product to market, and unique expertise of the licensee argue for a greater portion going to the licensee. Factors such as low risk of commercialization, small capital investments to bring the product to market, and numerous suitable licensees argue for a greater portion going to the licensor.

## Licensing Pending Patent Applications

The perplexity of valuing patent rights is compounded when the technology is not the subject of an issued patent but a pending one. The financial risk of establishing a royalty payment which fairly compensates the owner for the patent without unduly burdening commercialization is compounded by the uncertainty of the breadth of the hoped-for patent.

The payment of royalties can be tied to the milestone of a patent issuing to try to mitigate this risk. This simplistic approach, however, does more harm than good. After the licensing deal is signed, the patent applicant is motivated to quickly issue a patent from the pending application, even if the resulting patent is unduly narrow. In addition, when driving to quickly issue a patent, the applicant may make unnecessary concessions in the prosecution of the patent application (the negotiation with the U.S. Patent Office). These concessions may end up limiting the value of the patent by limiting the scope of the patent.

The risk to the licensee is significant. Upon signing the licensing deal, the licensee invests in the commercialization of a product, relying on the securing protection of the issued patent. Once the patent issues, the licensee often finds the patent provides only a narrow scope of protection. However, the licensor has been careful to include the commercial embodiment within the scope of the narrow patent. The licensee is thus faced with the choice of incurring the cost of redesigning the product to design around the narrow patent, with the attendant risk of a charge of bad faith from the licensor, or paying the royalty. If the product succeeds, competitors are free to design around the narrow patent, thus avoiding both the costs of royalty payments and the risks of the introduction of an innovative product.

However, entrepreneurial managers cannot wait for the patent to issue to enter into a licensing relationship. Delaying product introduction while the patent office processes the application — an average of two to three years — would put both licensees and licensors at a huge disadvantage against competitors that rely on in-house innovation. Moreover, lucrative licensing opportunities will be lost to competitors who are willing to incur the risk of licensing the pending applications.

The challenge of licensing a pending patent application is further compounded by the biases licensor and licensee bring to the negotiating table. Licensors — often the inventors of the technology — assume any patents that issue from the pending application will broadly reflect their own perceived importance of their innovation. Thus, the licensor often has an inflated view of the potential patent profit. On the other hand, the licensee often views paying a royalty as a nuisance payoff because of the threat that even a narrow patent will cover the commercial embodiment. Thus, the licensee often has a deflated view of the potential patent profit.

When the difficulty of financially defining the exclusionary power of a patent is compounded by the still-pending status of an application, many simply give up or resort to writing simplistic triggering milestones into the license agreement, such as the issuance of any patent. Simplistic valuation methods, which are inappropriate when applied even to issued patents, are an invitation to financial disaster when applied to pending applications. At least when applied to issued patents, the probability is minimized of licensing a narrow patent that does not justify a royalty payment in the narrow band defined by the industry norm. This is because the engineering, financial, and marketing professionals can relate the existing breadth of the patent to the implications of paying the industry royalty. In other words, when the cost of paying the royalty is compared to potential noninfringing substitute products, it is likely the project will not make financial sense. While still a problem because the opportunity will be lost, at least the firm will not overpay for the technology.

If a pending application is licensed based on the standard evaluation methods, overpayment is almost assured. Since the breadth of the patent does not directly enter into the analysis of a licensing opportunity, it will be assumed that whatever patent issues will justify payment of the standard royalty. With no existing exclusionary breadth against which to judge this royalty, licenses will be signed without even indirect consideration of the patent profit. Likewise, the opportunity to license and therefore exploit applications which issue as patents with a broad ability to exclude substitutes will be lost because enlightened competitors will outbid for the license by paying higher than the standard valuation methods.

## An Appropriate Valuation Method

By understanding and utilizing sound economic and financial principles to value pending applications, an appropriate financial basis for royalty payments and legal structure for licensing pending applications can be used. The appropriate foundation for defining a royalty in any patent license is the patent profit. Any licensing structure should directly tie the royalty payment to the exclusionary power of the patent.

In the basic embodiment of this structure, three milestone categories of possible royalty levels are built into the agreement. The amount of payment in each milestone category is tied to the scope of the issued patent. At the first milestone, a small nuisance royalty amount is set which addresses the licensee's fear of an extremely narrow patent that covers the licensee's commercial embodiment, but presents little patent profit. At the highest milestone, a royalty consistent with the licensor's inflated expectations will be paid in the unlikely event a broad pioneer patent issues. Thus, an agreement that embodies both the licensee's deflated expectations and the licensor's inflated expectations is signed, bridging this bias gap. Between these two milestones, the middle milestone represents the likely scope of the patent.

This middle milestone commands a royalty between the nuisance royalty expected by the licensee and the pioneer royalty expected by the licensor. In the likely event a patent in this middle milestone issues, the patent owner will receive a royalty payment that is not as great as his inflated bias but that reflects the licensor's inability to issue the pioneer patent. The licensee will pay a royalty payment that is not as small as his deflated bias, but that reflects a scope of protection which is greater than the narrow patent he feared.

As with any licensing relationship, this arrangement should be embodied in a sufficiently definitive legal structure to minimize the possibility of misunderstandings between the licensor and licensee. At the lowest milestone, the standard triggering milestone of issuance of any patent can be used. This works in this structure because the payment of a nuisance royalty is sufficiently small so that the actual coverage of a narrow patent is not critical. Payment of royalties in the remaining milestones ties to achievement of patent prosecution milestones. These milestones can be defined by the inclusion of actual claims in the license agreement. Thus, a broad pioneer claim defines the patent milestone that results in payment of the pioneer royalty while a claim setting forth the most likely scope defines the middle royalty milestone. These claims can be set forth as schedules to the license agreement.

The structure described above represents the simplest embodiment of this concept. The application of this concept can be as varied as the needs and creativity of the parties. For example, if focusing claim coverage on several different aspects of the invention is a viable strategy in prosecuting the patent, patent prosecution milestones can be defined around claims defining these different aspects. If a synergistic effect is sought by securing allowance of different claims directed towards different aspects, the royalty can be tied into the number of patent prosecution milestones achieved in addition to specific milestones. In addition, the consideration for achieving a patent milestone need not be solely tied to a royalty level. Lump sum payments or any other consideration can be tied to achievement of patent prosecution milestones.

## An Example of Valuation

A fanciful case study involving a pending application directed to toasted corn flakes demonstrates these principles. The patent applicant desires to license the pending application to a food product company. The patent applicant and the company agree that if no patent issues and therefore perfect substitute products exist, the product will sell for $1.80, of which $0.80 will be the economic profit. If a broad pioneer patent issues, the parties agree that the product could be sold for $2.30, with the $0.50 difference representing the patent profit. The parties believe a narrow patent would enable a small $0.05 patent profit with a resulting $1.85 selling price.

The patent applicant (licensor) believes any patent that issues from the pending application will be a pioneer patent covering all cold cereal products, including not only toasted corn flakes but also puffed rice. This inflated view of the value of the potential patent results in a ten percent royalty demand. Fearful of the issuance of a narrow patent that covers only the particular toasted corn flakes product, the other company (licensee) has a deflated view of the value of the potential patent and makes a one percent royalty offer. The licensee compromises and agrees to pay a two-percent royalty if any patent that covers the commercial product issues. The licensor compromises and agrees to an eight-percent royalty if a pioneer claim issues. An example of such a claim, which is to be attached to the agreement as a schedule tied into a milestone provision, is a food product comprised of a grain-based cereal which has been processed sufficiently to enable consumption without any further processing at all.

The middle milestone is defined by a royalty of five percent for issuance of a claim whose scope is between the top and bottom milestones. An example of such a claim, which is to be attached to the agreement as a schedule tied into a milestone provision, is a food product comprising a corn-based cereal toasted sufficiently to enable consumption without further heat processing. This middle milestone is not as broad as the pioneer patent. Where as the pioneer claim applies to all grains and processing, the middle milestone applies only to corn-based products and heat processing; however, it is broader than a patent that covers only the commercial product.

Licensing in this way effectively manages the risk of licensing pending applications. It also bridges the gap between the natural biases of the licensor and licensee. Finally, this structure decreases the potential for conflict between the licensor and the licensee because the financial payment is more closely tied to the true economic value of the patent.

## CHAPTER 6

# PATENT CHARTING

George made a major decision regarding the future direction of his company. Finally convinced that he would never get around to commercializing the gargle-blaster technology in more distant applications, he decided to license out the technology to these applications. He also decided to expand his product line by licensing in a related technology, the commercialization of which would compliment his speaker sales.

With his experience in commercializing the gargle-blaster speakers, he felt comfortable using economic and financial principles in deciding on a fair royalty to license out his technology. However, he felt much less confident in valuing technology to license in. These technologies were even less advanced than the gargle-blaster and, while applications had been filed, patents were not expected to issue for at least two years.

George asked a patent attorney to perform stages one and two due diligence to ensure that title to the technology and applications was clear and to explore whether the exploitation of the technology could infringe on third party rights. It was about the third stage (valuing the intellectual property) that George was concerned.

In order to get a valuation, George had Chip perform due diligence into the technology in engineering, Mildred in marketing, and one of his consultants,

Jennifer Law, in finance. George brought Chip, Mildred, and Jennifer together with his patent attorney to present their findings.

As the discussions droned on, George wished they had a framework through which they could focus their discussions in trying to understand the value of these potential patents. When he expressed his frustration about the lack of a framework, Jennifer related that when she was with BigCo, she had been part of a due diligence team that used a technique called "patent charting." This technique used a simple graphical representation of the patent rights in order to understand these issues. This chapter builds such a model, referred to as a "patent chart."

## Using a Patent Chart

A patent chart has numerous uses. It gives an overview of the technology in the field, while magnified "windows" can show small sections of the chart in greater detail. It illustrates the scope of the exclusivity of patents as well as showing overlapping claims and areas of possible conflict. It can show the likelihood and extent of mutually blocking patents. All this information is useful, not only in potential licensing situations, but also when making decisions about the directions of research and development or whether to apply for a patent for a new development.

It is important to remember, however, that the patent chart is a visual aid only. It creates a simplified representation of the complexities of the scope and exclusivity of related patents, making it easier to sense "the whole picture." It is not mathematically exact, but only a fair approximation of the relationships between patents. It can be used to quickly pinpoint areas of possible conflict or broad exclusivity, but should never be used to make hard conclusions about these areas. Such conclusions can only be made through careful examination of the patent claims themselves.

## Setting Up the Chart

Initially, the state of technological development is represented on a two-dimensional surface. This representation is referred to as a "technology chart." The technology chart can be narrowed to focus on a particular field of technology. For example, a fairly large area of the chart could depict the state of the art of consumer audio. A smaller area would show the state of the art of speakers (see fig. 6-1).

In the same way, the current state of the art of a particular technological field can be seen on a separate page showing only part of the technology chart. Increasingly narrower fields of technology are depicted by increasingly smaller areas. Related technological fields are located in horizontal proximity. These related fields are shown either by small areas that show just the particular technological field or by larger areas that show several related technological fields.

A discrete spot on the technology chart represents a specific embodiment of technology. This specific embodiment, which aligns with the concept of prior art, can be an actual commercial product, a description of a device in the specification of a patent, a description in a technical article, or any other suitable disclosure. For example, a discrete spot on the consumer audio technology area represents a commercial audio receiver product.

The vertical axis of the technology chart shows the progression of technology: the bottom of the chart reflects past technological developments; the top of the chart is reserved for future, as yet unknown technological developments; and the middle of the chart reflects the current state of technology. Technological improvements occur over time; however, distances on the vertical axis do not represent increments of time but degrees of technological improvement, with large jumps in technology represented by large distances and minor improvements represented by short distances. Because any given area only shows a limited range in the progression of a particular technology, the area must be "scrolled" downward to expose past technology. As the technology chart is scrolled downward, an increasing number of specific embodiments of technology are exposed. As future technological developments occur, the increasingly crowded area will need be scrolled upward to show future developments.

The particular value of the technology chart lies in depicting the scope of patents. Initially, the "best mode" described in the patent specification is shown on the technology chart as a discrete spot, such as: X. Additionally, preexisting technology is shown below the patent description as a number of discrete spots.

## Charting the Scope of Patents

An ellipse represents the scope of patents. This ellipse functions similarly to a Venn circle.[1] To a large extent claims, can be fashioned to artfully avoid the prior art and thus their representation should be more fluid than a circle, but the claims must have a degree of continuity which is better represented by an ellipse. Additionally, the size of the ellipse is limited not only by preexisting technology, but also by the requirement that the specification must provide "support" for the claim.[2] Thus, even with artful lawyering, claims of unlimited scope cannot be fashioned.

For a patent to be valid, the scope of exclusivity cannot encompass prior art. On the technology chart, the patent ellipse representing exclusivity must not encompass any preexisting prior art. In addition, to satisfy the nonobviousness standard, the patent ellipse must be capable of obtaining a certain minimum size without encompassing prior art. When discussing patentability with managers, it is helpful to view lack of novelty as an extreme case of obviousness.[3] This simplifying fusion of these two concepts — nonobviousness and novelty — is used herein, often under the helpful European term "inventive step."

Because the patent ellipse must be drawn to avoid the prior art, the size of the ellipse depends on the distance of the invention from the prior art. The size of the ellipse also defines the scope of exclusivity reserved to the patent owner. Thus, narrow patents are represented by small ellipses. An example is a new noise elimination algorithm that slightly improves on a preexisting noise elimination algorithm. Even if the innovation is nonobvious and thus entitled to a patent, the scope of exclusivity is narrow.

## Pioneer Patents

At the opposite end of the spectrum are so-called "pioneer patents." Pioneer patents refer to patents covering large inventive steps that result in a broad scope covering a wide range of functional equivalents.[4] Pioneer patents are represented by large ellipses. An example is new digital storage that uses a radically different approach to store extremely high-quality digital sound in a fraction of the storage space. Because a pioneer patent represents a large advance in technology, the scope of exclusivity is broad and covers a wide range of functional equivalents.

Marvin Industries' gargle-blaster patent (fig. 6-1) is seen as an example of patent charting in the audio speaker technology. Several preexisting Xs represent prior art speakers, technology articles, and patent descriptions. The gargle-blaster system uses sophisticated digital compression software to allow significant miniaturization of audio speakers while retaining an extremely high quality of sound. The gargle-blaster technology is marked by a new X above the preexisting Xs in the same technological field. In defining the scope of exclusivity for this invention, the ellipse must be drawn to avoid encompassing any preexisting Xs. If this ellipse is able to achieve a minimum size while avoiding prior art Xs, the innovation is nonobvious and patent protection is available.

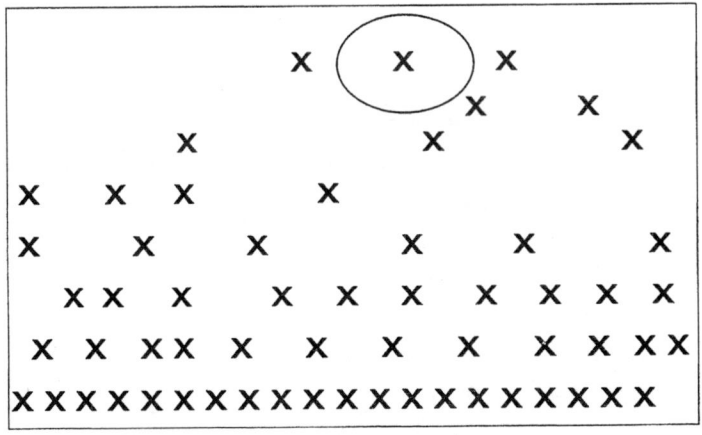

**Fig. 6-1. The Gargle-Blaster Patent**

The scope of a pioneer patent can be sufficiently broad to cover not only devices from the same narrow technological field, but also devices in adjacent related technological fields. For example, the patent on the gargle-blaster could cover not only speakers, but also use of the compression software in any environment. Likewise, the scope of exclusivity is limited not only by the vertical distance on the chart representing the improvement over prior art in the same technological field, but also by the horizontal proximity of prior art in related technological fields. For example, if the invention in the gargle-blaster recognized use of preexisting compression software in speakers, the scope of exclusivity would be limited by the prior art uses of the compression software. As seen in figure 6-1, prior art from related fields is represented by the Xs on either side of the X marking the invention.

## Other Uses of the Chart

In addition to the concept of availability and scope of patent protection, patent charting also can be used to depict infringements. If the patent reads on an infringing device, an X' representing that later device is encompassed by the ellipse defining the patent exclusivity of the first device (fig. 6-2).

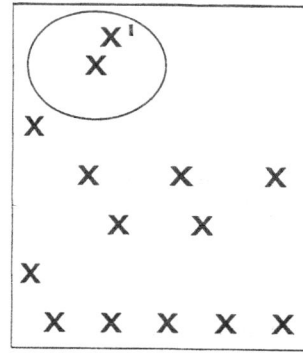

**Fig. 6-2. Infringment**

With only slightly increased complexity, the patent chart can represent additional patent principles. For example, most patents do not employ a single independent claim. Rather, they employ a series of both broad independent and narrower dependent claims. An X represents best-mode embodiment of the invention. A dependent claim is represented by a small ellipse surrounding the X. This small ellipse is encompassed by a large ellipse representing the independent claim, thus showing the narrowness of the dependent claim (fig. 6-3). Several dependent claims can be represented by several ellipses, all of which are smaller than the larger ellipse representing the independent claim.

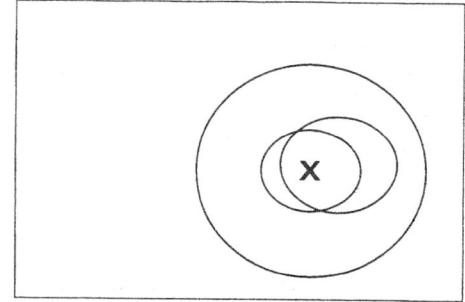

**Fig. 6-3. Claims of Varying Scope**

By utilizing these principles, the strategy of "patent flooding" can be charted. Patent flooding refers to a series of narrow patents on closely related embodiments of a technology. Even if a broad patent is not available, the "flooder" hopes to gain a broad scope of exclusivity by effectively combining several narrow patents (fig. 6-4).

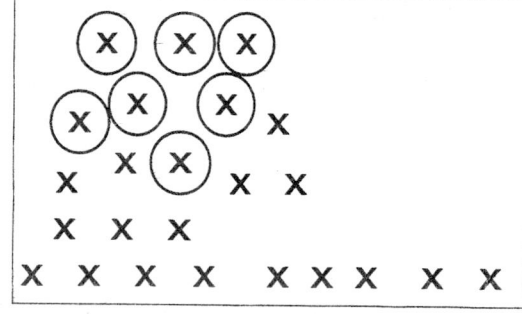

**Fig. 6-4. Patent Flooding**

Patent charting also can be used to clarify one of the most confusing concepts in the law of patents: the difference between patentability and infringement. A patent gives the patent owner the right to exclude others from making, using, or selling what is within the scope of the claims. The patent does not give the patent owner the affirmative right to commercialize the invention.[5] Thus, patentability is a separate issue from infringement.

## Mutually Blocking Patents

A patent can be obtained for an invention when that invention is a sufficient inventive step over the prior art. Any patent ellipses that may surround a prior X do not come into play in assessing patentability. If a preexisting ellipse from a prior invention encompasses the invention, commercialization of the invention infringes that prior patent. Thus, the owner of the prior patent can preclude the owner of the later patent from practicing in the area encompassed by the prior ellipse, even if the later patent likewise encompasses the area. The prior patent is said to "dominate" the later patent. (See Case Study: Patent Charting the Infant Radio Industry, below.)

Likewise, the owner of the later patent can preclude the owner of the prior patent from commercializing the innovation in the area encompassed by the later ellipse, even though the prior ellipse also encompasses this area. When this occurs, the patents are said to mutually block each other.[6] If the two patents are owned by different entities, only by cross-license can a product in the overlapping area be commercialized. Continuing a prior example, if the invention in the gargle-blaster recognized use of preexisting compression software in speakers, the $X_2$ seen in figure 6-5 could represent the gargle-blaster technology, while the $X_1$ could represent the original compression software. The owner of the patent on the digital compression invention could stop use in any environment,

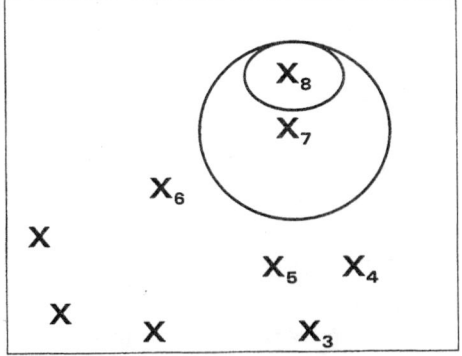

**Fig. 6-5. Mutually Blocking Patents**

including speakers, while the owner of the gargle-blaster patent could stop use by anyone in speakers, including the owner of the patent on the digital compression invention.

## The Doctrine of Equivalents

As with the distinction between the issues of patentability and infringement, the doctrine of equivalents is often misunderstood. Under this doctrine, even if the language of the claim does not literally describe or "read on" the potentially infringing device under investigation, if "insubstantial differences" exist between the language of the claims and the accused product, infringement can be present.[7]

On a technology chart, if an $X^1$ of a later device clearly falls within the ellipse of exclusivity of an earlier patent, literal infringement is clear (see fig. 6-2).[8] If the $X^1$ embodying the later device clearly falls outside the ellipse, no infringement is present. When the $X^1$ of the later device lies close to the border of the ellipse, however, the issue of infringement is more difficult. In this case, additional investigation amplifies and better defines where the border of the ellipse lies. This additional investigation can include arguments the patent owner made to the patent office when gaining allowance of the patent,[9] the preexisting technology over which the patent was allowed,[10] and even expert opinion about the scope of the patent.[11] These factors define the scope of the doctrine of equivalents.

Graphically, the line that forms the ellipse must be magnified to expose in better detail the bounds of exclusivity. The magnified depiction discloses not the single solid line seen from a distance, but rather a band of "gray area." If upon enlargement the $X^1$ representing the later device clearly falls within or outside of the gray area, the additional study has determined whether or not infringement exists (fig. 6-6). However, the practical reality is that the $X^1$ of the later device can still fall within the gray area, where neither a clear infringement nor a clear noninfringement exists. In other words, this gray area represents situations where reasonable minds can differ on whether infringement exists.

A corollary of the doctrine of equivalents is the "reverse doctrine of equivalents." Under this doctrine, even if the claims seem to literally read on the device under investigation, if the device is so far changed that it performs the function in a substantially different way, infringement may not be present.[12] Graphically, this is represented on a technology chart (fig. 6-6) by an $X^1$, which at first appears to be within the ellipse of exclusivity but upon magnification falls outside the gray area.

The particular shape and width of the gray area is defined by the arguments of the patent owner in gaining allowance, the location of the preexisting technology, and expert opinion. Upon further study the shape and width of the gray area is made

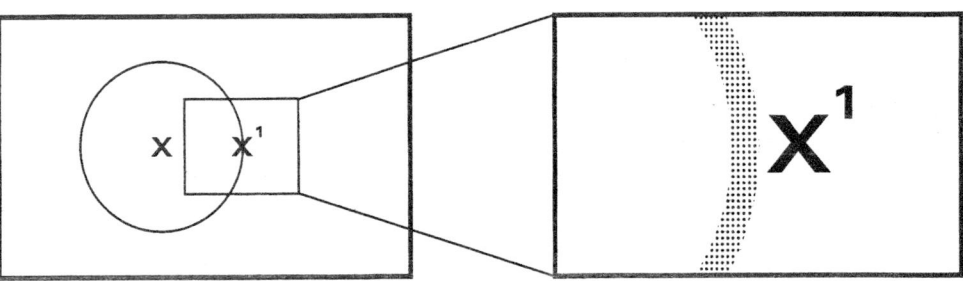

**Fig. 6-6. Patent Chart Detail – Noninfringement**

more and more clear, although the existence of a gray area of some width may always be present.

## Conclusion

Returning to George Marvin's meeting, a patent chart is presented that shows the patents, the closest prior art, and any potentially blocking patents. The patent attorney directs the discussion regarding the strengths, weaknesses, and scopes of the patents. Chip is quizzed about the potential and viability of alternative technologies, including manufacturing costs. Mildred opines about the marketplace acceptance of the technology and the alternative technologies, and what, if any, pricing premium could be charged for the target technology. Jennifer digests this information to calculate the value of the target's technology and patents. This discussion provides an education to the entrepreneurial manager about the potential value of the patent.

This is only one example of when patent charting is useful. A second example lies in strategic decisions on areas to focus research and development funds. Often, research and development projects are completed only to discover the existence of blocking patents. Patent charting helps entrepreneurial managers avoid this problem when assigning research and development expenditures.

A decision to explore a potential research project is made. As a first step, a patent attorney completes a broad-based investigation of the patent rights in this field of technology, including a state of the art study. A patent chart is created that graphically represents the existing patent rights in the field. Once again, the patent attorney presents his or her findings to professionals from engineering, finance, and marketing, who have completed their own due diligence. The patent chart enables the group to identify areas to avoid because of the existence of blocking patents owned by competitors, areas where developments will not be blocked by existing patents, and areas where noncompeting parties have developed expertise and rights which may be available for license or joint development.

While the preceding examples demonstrate the value of technological charting in complex areas, it is also useful in less complex inquiries. The decision of whether to incur the expense of seeking patent protection for a new development depends on the scope of available exclusivity. Charting the new development against existing technology will educate entrepreneurial managers to the likely scope of the patent. Whether an existing patent can be designed around depends on the scope of the patent and availability of alternative technologies. A detailed patent chart can demonstrate the likelihood of being able to design around a patent successfully.

These represent just some of the uses of patent charting techniques. From presenting detailed results of complex noninfringement studies to impromptu discussions on patentability, use of the patent charting techniques outlined in this chapter results in better decision-making when managing technology.

## Patent Charting the Infant Radio Industry

The experience of the U.S. radio industry at its infancy and the invention and development of the vacuum tube in particular is illustrated by use of patent charting.[13] Entrepreneurial managers in the e-commerce field may recognize parallels between the case study, which involved a "technology race" in an infant industry, and the technology races underway in the e-commerce industry today.

The conception of the radio industry occurred when Guglielmo Marconi, an Italian physicist, first carried out successful experiments with wireless telegraphy in 1894. The basic U.S. patent on radio was granted to Marconi in 1897.[14] This patent helped make Marconi's company, Marconi Wireless Telegraph Co., an early leader in the emerging U.S. radio industry. At this early stage, the radio industry was primarily dedicated to commercial uses such as ship-to-shore communications. While Marconi also worked on an early crude receiver, the high frequency combined with the low energy level of the radio waves posed a particular challenge to receiving radio waves.

In 1905, Marconi acquired rights to U.S. Patent No. 803,684, titled "Instrument for Converting Alternating Electric Currents into Continuous Currents" and invented by Sir John Ambrose Fleming of Great Britain. This patent described an electrical component consisting of a glass container having a partial vacuum, two separate terminals within the glass container, and a circuit outside the glass container connected to the two terminals.[15] The component was designed to detect high frequency oscillations such as radio waves.

Detection was achieved by permitting current to flow in one direction only, from the hot first terminal to the cold second terminal. This modified current could then be interpreted by further electronic components. While referred to at the time as a detector, this device became known as a vacuum tube diode. When an electrode is heated in a vacuum, the electrode emits surface electrons. If another electrode is close by, an electrical field is created between the heated electrode and the cold electrode by the attraction of the emitted surface electrons to the cold electrode. This results in a current flow through the vacuum. If the polarity of the electrical signal is reversed, no current flows. Thus, the diode allows current to flow in one direction but blocks current flow in the reverse direction. This property can be used to rectify alternating current.[16]

The closest prior art to the Fleming patent was Thomas Edison's 1884 U.S. Patent No. 307,031, titled "Electrical Indicator." Edison's patent disclosed the so-called "Edison effect" exploited in Edison's incandescent electric light bulb. The Edison effect results when a hot terminal and a cold terminal are provided with electrical current flowing from the hot to the cold terminal. When an incandescent filament is used, light results. However, Edison in no way recognized or predicted the particular application Fleming designed in his vacuum tube diode.

Prior to Fleming's invention of the vacuum tube diode, other attempts had been made to produce a commercially feasible detector. These devices included a coherer, a microphone, a magnetic detector, the Schumaker cell, and a crystal detector. Thus, these devices helped define the state of the technology against which the patentability of Fleming's invention was judged.

The coherer was a tube filled with metal filings. When high frequency oscillations were applied to the ends of the tube, the filings would coalesce. The coalescence of the metal filings allowed passage of a current provided by a local battery. This current could be detected by electronic components. Capable of detecting only strong radio waves, the coherer had to be shaken after receipt of a signal to restore the loose metal filings to the receiving position. This limitation offered obvious disadvantages.

The microphone used a loose contact between two dissimilar terminals, such as carbon and steel. Upon receipt of high frequency oscillations, the contact resistance between the two terminals would change. This change could be detected by electronic components. The microphone was extremely delicate and extremely difficult to adjust.

The magnetic detector used a moving band of soft iron passing in front of magnets that magnetized the iron. High frequency oscillations demagnetized the soft iron band. These high frequency oscillations could be detected by electronic components. This magnetic detector was widely used before the invention of the vacuum tube, but was extremely insensitive.

The Schumaker cell used a cell containing an electrolyte solution having two immersed electrodes. High frequency oscillations were picked up by the electrolyte solution and detected by the electrodes. This arrangement functioned quite well as long as the cell was absolutely still. While this device was extremely sensitive, the disadvantage to its use on ships is obvious.

The crystal detector used the contact between a crystal — such as silicon — and a fine metallic wire. Upon receipt of high frequency oscillations, the contact between the crystal and the wire produced a self-restoring high resistance that rectified and demodulated the radio waves. While this device achieved the most commercial success of any of these prior art detectors, it was undependable, lacked sensitivity, and required constant adjustment of the wire-to-crystal contact.

These devices were closely related in that each tried to solve the same technological hurdle as the vacuum diode. However, none of these achieved any satisfactory level of performance. Because of these poor results, none of these devices was more than a minor advance in technology. Thus, the prior art at the time Fleming invented his device consisted of two general categories. The first category consisted of the devices from the same field designed specifically to detect high frequency oscillations. None of these devices functioned nearly as satisfactorily as Fleming's invention. In

CASE
STUDY

CONT.

fact, only the best of these prior devices sustained any degree of commercial feasibility and all were replaced by use of the vacuum tube. It is clear Fleming's invention consisted of a large inventive step over these crude prior art devices.

The second category consisted of prior art in adjacent technological fields, the closest of which was the Edison patent. While the Edison patent described generally the Edison effect used in Fleming's invention, nothing in Edison's disclosure suggested application of the Edison effect to detecting high frequency oscillations. In fact, the Edison patent discussed the Edison effect nearly 20 years before the time Fleming applied it in his invention. This factor combined with the long-felt need for this type of device are strong indications of patentability.

With this background, Fleming's vacuum tube diode can be plotted on a technology chart. Initially, we plot the various detectors that predated the Fleming device: the "coherer" is designated $X_1$; the microphone $X_2$; the magnetic detector $X_3$; the Schumaker cell $X_4$; and the crystal detector $X_5$ (fig. 6-7). While all can be grouped closely together, the crystal detector attained some level of commercial applicability while the Schumaker cell operated most effectively. Thus, these two devices are located higher than those that failed.

We add the Edison patent to the chart next. The Edison effect employed more advanced technology than the prior detectors and is therefore located above the crude detector devices. However, the Edison effect was not recognized as applicable to detecting high frequency oscillations, so it is located vertically above, but horizontally offset from, the prior detectors ($X_6$).

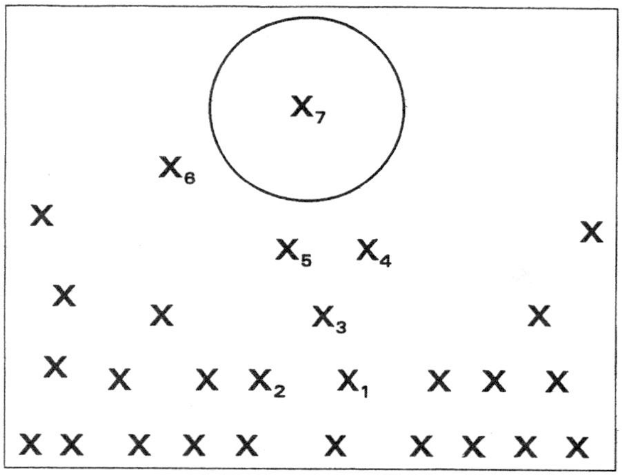

Fig. 6-7. Vacuum Tube Diode

We now add the Fleming vacuum diode to the technology chart. Because the Fleming device was designed for the same purpose as, but was superior to the crude prior art detectors, it is located at a distance vertically above these detectors. However, even though the $X_6$ representing the Edison effect is located above the crude detectors, because it is horizontally offset from Fleming's vacuum diode, an ellipse of significant size can be drawn around Fleming's invention ($X_7$), while still avoiding the Edison patent. Through the exercise of patent charting, an intuitive appreciation of the broad scope and thus the value of the Fleming patent is gained. The Fleming vacuum diode represented a significant technological improvement and therefore was entitled to a broad scope of patent exclusivity.

Fleming described his new invention before the Royal Society of Britain in February 1905. Dr. Lee DeForest saw the publication of this presentation in the United States. DeForest — sometimes called "the father of radio" — had a prolific career which included more than 300 inventions in radio and related technologies. After exposure to Fleming's theory, DeForest's work began to increasingly parallel Fleming's disclosure until, in an address to the American Institute of Electrical Engineers in October 1906, DeForest described in different terminology what was essentially the Fleming vacuum-tube diode.[17]

DeForest went on to develop a three-electrode detector he referred to as the "P.N. type Audion DeForest Detector." Technological improvements associated with this device were patented in three U.S. patents: U.S. Patent No. 824,637, issued 26 June 1906; U.S. Patent No. 836,070, issued 13 November 1906; and U.S. Patent No. 879,532, issued 18 February 1908.[18] DeForest's device now is better known as the vacuum tube triode or amplifier.

This device consisted of a glass container having a partial vacuum, a hot terminal and a separate second cold terminal contained in the glass container, and a grid-like wire filament located between the cold terminal and the hot terminal. Detection by rectifying the high frequency oscillations was achieved by permitting current to flow from the cold terminal to the filament and from the hot terminal to the filament, in one direction only. By placing a control grid between the hot and the cold terminals of the diode, the flow of electrons could be controlled. This control was used to amplify the rectified high-frequency electronic signal.

The vacuum tube triode was of major commercial importance to detecting high-frequency oscillations. The device made it possible to amplify radio waves before interpretation by further electronic components. This allowed use of much weaker signals, which allowed for much longer-distance reception. DeForest's patents on the vacuum tube triode were eventually sold to American Telephone & Telegraph Co., whose purchase of the DeForest patents was motivated by AT&T's concern over the competitive threat radio posed to its telephone market.

DeForest's invention was a huge commercial success and formed the basis for receiving all transmitted signals, including high-fidelity radio and television, up to and beyond the invention of the transistor in 1947. While integrated circuits have all but replaced the vacuum tube triode today, it is still found in some high-powered amplification.

Clearly, the vacuum tube triode was patentable over the prior art. On the patent chart, DeForest's three-element triode is placed above the prior detectors, including Fleming's two-element diode. But because the Fleming two-element diode was close prior art, the DeForest device was not entitled to a large scope of exclusivity. This is plotted on the technology chart in figure 6-8, with DeForest's triode designated $X_8$ and the scope of DeForest's patents represented by the surrounding ellipse.

CASE STUDY CONT.

This, of course, is not the end of the story. For determining patentability, the existence and location of prior ellipses are not relevant. Thus, DeForest was awarded a patent on his vacuum tube triode because it involved an inventive step over the Fleming device. However, the bad news for DeForest was that Fleming's ellipse of exclusivity was sufficiently broad to encompass his vacuum tube triode. Thus, commercialization of the vacuum tube triode infringed Fleming's vacuum tube diode patent. The bad news for Marconi Wireless was that, even though the vacuum tube triode offered significant commercial advantages over the vacuum tube diode, DeForest's patents prevented Marconi Wireless' commercialization of the vacuum tube triode.

Figure 6-8 depicts the situation after court resolution of the dispute between Marconi and DeForest.[19] Prior to trial, Marconi Wireless even admitted that its three-element detector infringed DeForest's patents on the vacuum tube triode. After trial, the district court determined DeForest's three-element detector infringed Fleming's broad vacuum tube diode patent. This decision was affirmed on appeal.[20]

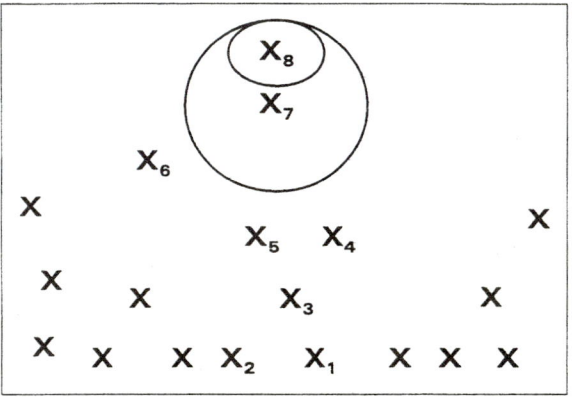

Fig. 6-8. Mutually Blocking Vacuum Tube Patents

Without some form of cross-license, both companies were precluded from making, using, or selling the vacuum tube triode, and of course, no one else could make, use, or sell the vacuum tube triode in the United States. Through use of its vacuum tube diode at the end of World War I, Marconi Wireless was the only company in the United States capable of handling commercial transatlantic radio communication. General Electric, by virtue of its control of patents to the electronic alternator that made long-range signal transmission possible, also staked out a position in the infant U.S. radio industry. Likewise, Westinghouse staked out a position with its control of patents for improvements to the additional receiving circuitry to which the detected signal was connected.

These patent conflicts, which arose due to the rapid growth of this infant industry, were one of the factors which helped lead to the creation of the Radio Corporation of America in 1919. Another factor was the U.S. government's concern that Marconi Wireless was entirely owned by the British Marconi concern, Marconi Wireless Telegraph Co., Ltd. In fact, in a patent investigation in 1919, the Navy found that not "a single company among those making radio sets for the Navy possessed basic patents sufficient to enable them to supply, without infringement, ... a complete transmitter or receiver."[21] While the situation that no U.S. company could use the vacuum tube triode was unsatisfactory, the firms involved apparently lacked sufficient motivation to cross-license. By virtue of its right to use and exclude others from use of Fleming's vacuum tube diode, Marconi Wireless was still the only U.S. firm capable of transatlantic radio communications. This position enabled Marconi Wireless to profit handsomely.

Given the potential effect on the country's defense, the situation was ripe for government intervention. At the prompting of Franklin D. Roosevelt, then Under Secretary of the Navy, the General Electric Corporation formed the Radio Corporation of America (RCA) to acquire the assets of Marconi Wireless. This was accomplished within one month of RCA's incorporation.

General Electric and RCA entered into a cross-license covering each other's radio patents. A year later, American Telephone & Telegraph bought a major position in RCA and cross-licensed its radio patents with RCA. By 1920, the logjam between the Fleming diode patent and the DeForest triode patent was broken by pooling together RCA's and AT&T's patents. In 1921, Westinghouse also joined the pool, buying a position in and licensing its patents to RCA in exchange for RCA selling Westinghouse equipment.

The application of the U.S. patent law principles that resulted in the most famous instance of mutual blocking patents is better understood through patent charting. As the second entry to this technology, DeForest was precluded from marketing the vacuum tube triode. While DeForest would argue he should not be precluded from using his invention, DeForest's use of Fleming's principles could not be ignored. Without Fleming's work on the vacuum tube diode, would DeForest have derived the vacuum tube triode? By virtue of his late-arriving improvement over the vacuum tube diode, should DeForest have been allowed to profit without giving Fleming his due?

In fact, the primary loss from these mutually blocking patents was to society. While superior radios were available outside the United States, as a result of the patent situation only radios of inferior capability were available within. The situation was ripe for governmental intervention, such as Navy Secretary Roosevelt's patent-pooling resolution. That resolution extracted a future toll. By virtue of its government-endorsed acquisition of virtually all radio technology, RCA soon enjoyed a dominant position — too dominant, the government decided. In a classic turnabout, RCA and the Department of Justice engaged in a string of antitrust disputes as a result of RCA's dominant position.

The major event in this antitrust battle was an antitrust lawsuit filed against RCA by the Justice Department in 1930. When the suit was settled, General Electric, AT&T, and Westinghouse were forced to sell their interests in RCA. The circle was completed in 1986 when, with the Justice Department's approval, General Electric again purchased RCA.

CASE
STUDY

CONT.

## Endnotes

1. Eugene A. Avallone et al., *Marks Standard Handbook for Mechanical Engineers* 9th ed. (New York: McGraw Hill, 1988), 2-2, 2-3.

2. *In re Hyatt*, 708 F. 2d 712 (Fed. Cir. 1983).

3. *Connell v. Sears, Roebuck & Co.*, 722 F. 2d 1542, 1548 (Fed. Cir. 1983). "[A] disclosure that anticipates under *Patents*, Title 35, U.S. CODE, §102 also renders the claim invalid under Ibid., §103, for 'anticipation is the epitome of obviousness'."

4. *Westinghouse v. Boyden Brake*, 170 U.S. 537 (1898).

5. *Atlas Powder Co. v. E.I. DuPont de Nemours & Co.*, 750 F. 2d 1569,1580 (Fed. Cir. 1984). "A patent is not the grant of a right to make or use or sell. It does not, directly or indirectly, imply any such right. It grants only the right to exclude others."

6. *Rolls-Royce, Ltd. v. GTE Valeron Corp.*, 800 F. 2d 1101, 1110 n.9 (Fed. Cir. 1986). "[T]hat someone has a patent right to exclude others from making the invention claimed in his patent does not mean that his invention cannot infringe claims of another patent broad enough to encompass, i.e. to 'dominate' his invention."

7. *Warner-Jenkinson Co., Inc. v. Hilton Davis Chemical Co.*, 520 U.S. 17, 31 (1997).]

8. *Mannesmann Demag Corp. v. Engineered Metal Products Co.*, 793 F. 2d 1279, 1283 (Fed. Cir. 1986) "Literal infringement requires that the accused device embody every element of the patent claim …."

9. *Howes v. Medical Components, Inc.*, 814 F. 2d 638 (Fed. Cir. 1987).

10. *Wilson Sporting Goods Co. v. David Geoffrey & Assoc.*, 904 F. 2d 677 (Fed. Cir.), *cert. denied*, 498 U.S. 992 (1990).

11. *Snellman v. Ricoh Co.*, 862 F. 2d 283 (Fed. Cir. 1988), *cert. denied*, 491 U.S. 910 (1989).

12. *Graver Tank & Manufacturing Co. v. Linde Air Products Co.*, 339 U.S. 605 (1950).

13. For background on the origins of the radio industry, see G. Sturney, *The Economic Development of Radio* (London: G. Duckworth, 1958); Hugh G.L. Aitken et al., *The Origins of Radio* (New York: Wiley, 1976); William K. MacLaurin, *Invention and Innovation in the Radio Industries* (New York: McMillan, 1949).

14. U.S. Patent No. 586,193, issued 13 July 1897, and later reissued as Re. 11,913 on 4 June 1901.

15. Claim 1, representative of the diode patent claims, provided: "The combination of a vacuous vessel, two conductors adjacent to but not touching each other in the vessel, means for heating one of the conductors, and a circuit outside the vessel connecting the two conductors."

16. While Fleming did not himself have this precise understanding of the way in which his vacuum diode operated at the time of invention, his patent satisfied the requirement that the inventor describe the invention adequately to enable one skilled in the art to duplicate the invention. See *Newman v. Quigg*, 877 F. 2d 1575 (Fed. Cir. 1989), *cert. denied*, 495 U.S. 932 (1990).

17. *Marconi Wireless Telegraph Co. v. DeForest Radio Telephone & Telegraph Co.*, 236 F. 942 (D.N.Y. 1916), *aff'd*, 243 F. 560 (2d Cir. 1917) and *Marconi Wireless Telegraph Co. v. DeForest Radio Telephone & Telegraph Co.*, 243 F. 560 (2d Cir. 1917).

18. Claim 2 of DeForest's U.S. Patent No. 879,532, which is representative of the triode patent claims, provided: "An oscillation detector comprising an evacuated vessel, two electrodes enclosed within said vessel, means for heating one of said electrodes, and a conducting member enclosed within said vessel and interposed between said electrodes."

19. *Marconi Wireless Telegraph Co. v. DeForest Radio Telephone & Telegraph Co.*, 236 F. 942 (D.N.Y. 1916).

20. *Marconi Wireless Telegraph Co. v. DeForest Radio Telephone & Telegraph Co.*, 243 F. 560 (2d Cir. 1917).
21. Federal Trade Commission, *Report of the Federal Trade Commission on the Radio Industry in Response to House Resolutions 548*, 67th Cong., 4th sess., 1 December 1923, 25.

# INFRINGEMENT

George Marvin didn't quite know what to make of the letter. While it did not sound threatening, it was obviously not good news that a competitor's attorney was informing him of "a patent that should be reviewed with respect to the gargle-blaster speakers." George wondered how this patent could relate to the gargle-blaster speakers and not have been found during Marvin's initial technological due diligence. He also wondered if this letter would affect his upcoming round of financing. Because sales of the gargle-blaster speakers were going great, he had high expectations for the success of this round. Finally, he had been expanding his manufacturing capacity so that cash flow was increasingly tight. George wondered if the money he would spend on his attorney investigating the letter would be better spent elsewhere. Still, the cautions of his attorney that "no due diligence is perfect due diligence" counseled him to make the call.

While receipt of a so-called "cease and desist" letter is never good news, many of these letters are written with little information on the actual technical workings in the accused product, so an entrepreneurial manager should not overreact to such a letter. However, the law creates a disincentive to aggressively word cease and desist letters on even a clear patent infringement, so the tone of the letter will not differentiate between true threats, fishing expeditions, or informative notices. Because of the enormity of a true threat, these letters should be investigated.

Due diligence into a letter of this type focuses on the two main defenses to patent infringement: noninfringement and invalidity. As with any due diligence, a reasoned approach involves researching these two defenses in stages. At the conclusion of each stage, two results can occur.

Either sufficient information has been uncovered to conclude a problem does not exist or more due diligence is required. Importantly, the conclusion that a problem does exist typically does not follow the conclusion of each stage. Rather, the conclusion a problem exists usually results from weighing the cost of further due diligence against the likelihood of finding that a problem does not exist and from weighing the financial scope of the problem.

## Noninfringement Inquiry

The fastest and least expensive inquiry is noninfringement. Thus, this analysis is often performed first. The patent itself should be reviewed to understand the technology and generally understand the scope of the claims. If the letter was written as a fishing expedition or as an informative notice, often the patent is clearly not infringed and the process can end. **Stage 1**

If the patent is read and the conclusion that the patent is not infringed cannot be reached, then more due diligence is required. Often, attorneys will unnecessarily alarm their clients by incorrectly characterizing the results of this first stage, leaving the client to conclude a problem exists. Again, the conclusion that a problem does exist should not follow this first stage.

Additional due diligence consists of more precisely defining the claims. Just as the intent of the parties to a contract can be determined by reviewing what happened during the contract negotiation, the prosecution history of the patent should be reviewed to better understand the scope of the patent. If the prosecution history shows the patent applicant specifically conceded a point that places the product outside the scope of the claims, the process can end. If the prosecution history is read and the conclusion that the patent is not infringed cannot be reached, then once again more due diligence is required. The conclusion a problem does exist should not follow the conclusion of this second stage. **Stage 2**

## Review of Prior Art

The next step is a review of the prior art over which the patent was allowed. The scope of the claims cannot be interpreted in such a way as to encompass the prior art. The prior art cited in the application is reviewed to determine whether the accused product is actually more similar to the prior art than to the patented technology. If the interpretation of the scope of the patent that encompasses the accused product also encompasses the prior art, the conclusion that the patent is not infringed can be reached. **Stage 3**

If the prior art is reviewed and the conclusion that the patent is not infringed cannot be reached, the prospects for the defense of noninfringement look bleak. However, even following the completion of these first three stages, it is premature to conclude that a problem exists. More due diligence is required, this time directed to the invalidity defense.

## Invalidity

Once issued, a patent is by law presumed valid. In issuing the patent, the patent examiner has rendered an opinion that the invention represents a nonobvious advance over the existing state of the technology. What if the examiner did not have the most relevant evidence concerning the state of the technology when passing judgment on the patent?

While a challenger to a patent carries the burden of invalidating the patent, this burden is more easily overcome when close prior art is found that the patent examiner did not consider in issuing the patent. If a single reference (source of prior art) discloses every element of an invention and was not considered by the examiner in allowing the patent, the burden of invalidating the patent can be overcome. Even if a single reference cannot be found, if a reference discloses nearly every element of the invention and was not considered by the examiner in allowing the patent, it can be combined with other prior art to demonstrate the obviousness of the invention. While more risky than a single reference, the burden of invalidating the patent can be overcome by combining more than one reference.

Thus, the next stage in analyzing a patent is to search for prior art the examiner did not consider in issuing the patent. Because prior art encompasses literally a worldwide range of possibilities, virtually unlimited resources can be expended in the proverbial search for the needle in the haystack. It is at this stage that the cost of further searching versus the likelihood of finding the information to conclude that a problem does not exist becomes the determining factor.

### Searching for Prior Art

Typically, the examiner searches patent office records to make this state-of-the-art determination. In some fields, such as pharmaceuticals, these records have a high probability of accurately reflecting the state of the technology. In some fields, like software and e-commerce, much of the evidence of the state of the art is not found in patent office records. However, important software patents have been invalidated by commercial products, offers for sale, promotional literature, advertisements, exhibits at a trade show, journal articles, and abstracts, and the search for these can yield fruitful results.

In addition, worldwide searching can often yield rewarding results. Examiners searching U.S. Patent Office records are limited in their ability to search the records of foreign patent offices, particularly for foreign language references. Hiring a patent expert to search these foreign haystacks can find the needle. Of course, the cost of searching every national patent office is huge. Thus, these searches often focus on patent offices where the local economy has a competitive advantage — for example, chemicals in Germany, electronics in Japan, and biotechnology in Scotland.

Prior art can also include public disclosure or commercial activity by the applicant or others that occurred more than one year before the application was filed. This can be an actual sale, conversations that might be viewed as offers for sale, public displays, exhibits at trade shows, articles in trade journals, or other public disclosure. Finding such commercial activity more than one year before the filing date of the patent can invalidate the patent.

## Disclosure

One further area of due diligence can also bear fruit. A patent applicant and other individuals involved in the application process have a duty to disclose to the patent office all information of which they are aware that is material to the patentability of the invention. Failure to meet this duty may render any issued patent unenforceable. While much evidence of this defense rests in the files of the patent owner and therefore cannot be reviewed before litigation, a surprising number of patents can be attacked based on publicly available evidence.

Many patent owners in the United States also file for equivalent patents in foreign countries. If prior art is cited by an examiner in another country but has not been cited in the U.S. Patent Office, the applicant has a duty to bring this to the examiner's attention. Thus, determining whether equivalent patents were filed can be the source of both pertinent prior art and, depending on the timing of the applications, evidence of a breach in the applicant's duty to disclose.

Even with these steps, often the likelihood of a court finding a patent infringed is probable rather than certain. Assessment of a charge of patent infringement necessarily involves balancing the risks and rewards of proceeding in view of of a competitor's patent. To weigh the risks and rewards, an entrepreneurial manager should understand the measure of damages available to the patent owner.

## The Measure of Damages

The headlines in the business press regarding infringement damages can be startling and intimidating.

- ▶ "Kodak to Pay Polaroid $925 Million to Settle Suit"
- ▶ "Jury Gives Litton $1.2 Billion in Honeywell Patent Dispute"
- ▶ "Microsoft to Pay Stac Judgment of $120 Million"

Implicit in any assessment of a claim of patent infringement is the balancing of the risks and rewards of proceeding in light of a patent. The threat of treble damages and attorneys' fees for "willfully" infringing a patent means that, in the absence of a good faith argument either that a patent is not infringed or is invalid, the patent must always be respected. At the opposite end of the spectrum, when a patent is clearly not infringed, threatening enforcement to bully a small, poorly funded competitor can expose the patent owner to antitrust liability. Unfortunately, ambiguity in the law combined with the unavailability of perfect information leaves a large gray area for the entrepreneurial manager. It is in this gray area, when the risk of a court finding a patent infringed is a probability rather than a certainty, that the risks and rewards of proceeding in light of a patent need to be weighed. In order to do this, an entrepreneurial manager should understand the measure of damages available to the patent owner.

While the award of damages in intellectual property litigation continues to grab the headlines of the business press, the primary remedy for infringement of intellectual property is an injunction prohibiting the infringing behavior. The entry of an injunction effectively stops the defendant from earning future profits on the sale of the infringing product and forfeits all the investments made in developing the product, which is by far the most significant financial impact of the infringement.

Injunctions come in three varieties: a temporary restraining order, a preliminary injunction, and a permanent injunction. As the names imply, both the temporary restraining order and the preliminary injunction are transitory, while the permanent injunction is forever. A temporary restraining order is designed to prevent the infringing behavior almost immediately upon filing an infringement action until a court hearing is held. A preliminary injunction is designed to prevent the infringing activity after the court hearing but before a trial on the merits. In addition to the probability of success on the merits, the key factors in determining whether such transitory relief is appropriate include whether a money award is sufficient to compensate the intellectual property owner and the preservation of the status quo — the status of the marketplace before the filing of the lawsuit.

In addition to an injunction, an intellectual property owner is sometimes entitled to an award of money damages. While money damages are typical in patent infringement cases, they are less typical in trademark cases. Unless the infringement involved deliberate deception, it is difficult to prove that consumers were actually confused into buying the wrong product.

In copyright cases damages are typical, either as proven damages or "statutory damages." These statutory damages provide an alternative damage measure in cases where actual damages cannot be proved. For each copyrighted work infringed, statutory damages range from $500 to $20,000, depending on factors such as "lost revenue" of the copyright owner and "expense saved and profits reaped" by the infringer.[1] Proof of willful infringement can increase the statutory damages to $100,000.

However, these statutory damages are only available to copyright owners who registered their copyright in a timely manner.[2]

## Patent Damages

In awarding damages in patent cases, the goal is to try to place the patent owner in the position they would have enjoyed had the infringement never taken place. A product sold under the protection of the exclusive grant of a patent enjoys a market in which perfect substitutes do not exist. If an infringing product is sold, a perfect substitute exists.

The effect of a perfect substitute in the marketplace is complex. Factors such as the pricing and marketing strategy of the infringer, the pricing and marketing responses by the patent owner, and even the reaction of other producers of noninfringing substitutes can have dramatic effects on the marketplace. Courts have recognized and developed new legal rules in addressing these factors.

The two principal measures of damages for infringement of a patent are royalty rate and lost profits. While still viewed as relevant evidence in limited circumstances, recovery of an infringer's profits was eliminated as a measure of damages in and of itself with the passage of the 1941 patent law. Because lost profits generally result in the greatest award for damages, patent owners try to prove this measure. Lost profits do not relate to the profits made by the infringer, but rather to the profits the patent owner would have made without the infringement. To the chagrin of many infringers, this measure often requires the infringer to pay more than the profits they made by selling the infringing devices, and can even result in the payment of significant damages if the infringing product lost money. In proving lost profits, four factors must be shown.

- ► Demand for the patented product.
- ► Absence of acceptable noninfringing substitutes.
- ► Capacity to meet the demand.
- ► The amount of profit that would have been made.[3]

In applying these factors, some courts have applied an inference that the patent owner lost sales equal in quantity to those actually made by the infringer. Some courts have applied a more limiting "market share" theory, under which the patent owner recovers lost sales damages based on that portion of the infringer's sales that corresponded to the patent owner's market share.[4]

Courts consider a list of factors that bear witness to the existence of the four main factors. Courts have found causation when the patent owner and the infringer are the "sole competitors in the marketplace,"[5] when the patent owner and the infringer bid against each other for contracts,[6] and when the infringer was a former customer of the patent owner.[7]

Courts have found causation lacking when the infringer charged a significantly lower price than the patent owner,[8] when the infringer sold to different markets than the patent owner,[9] and when noninfringing substitute products were available.[10] In this last category, courts have grappled with where to draw the line on what is and is not an adequate noninfringing substitute. The legal standard — "to be decreed acceptable, the alleged acceptable noninfringing substitute must not have a disparately higher price than or possess characteristics significantly different from the patented product" — offers little guidance.[11]

The difficulty courts have in grappling with proof of causation pales in comparison to the problem of where to draw the line on sales in calculating lost profits. When the patent is for an improvement, only covers a portion of the commercial product, or does not cover components sold with the patented product, courts struggle with what to include in calculating lost profits. Recently, courts have started to use sophisticated economic theories when calculating the amount of damages caused by the presence of the infringing product and compensating the patent owner for this damage.

For example, courts have awarded lost profits based not only on the sales price actually charged by the patent owner in competing against the infringing product, but also on what the price would have been had the infringing product not caused price erosion.[12] The price erosion theory can also apply to sales made by the patent owner for which the price eroded, and not just the sales by the infringer. Courts have been more reluctant to apply the price erosion theory to sales that have yet to be made, although in the right case such damages may well be included.[13] Of course, any award of lost profits based on price erosion should also account for any decline in demand that increased prices would have caused in this hypothetical world without competition from the infringing product.

A recent theory of calculating damages includes sales of nonpatented products that would have been sold by the patent owner if the infringing products had not been sold.[14] Like the razor blades in a patented razor, this theory in essence relies on the increase in sales of complementary products (the razor blade) when sales of the complemented product (the patented razor) increase. This theory, referred to as "convoy damages," has even gone so far as to award damages to a patent owner who did not even sell products covered by the patent, but who sold nonpatented products that competed against the infringer's products that were covered by the patent.[15]

If the patent owner cannot prove lost profits, the floor on damages is based on payment of a "reasonable royalty." This is often the case when the patent owner does not commercially exploit the patented technology. If the patent is subject to a licensing program, this royalty is based on the established royalty under that program. If lost profits cannot be proven and the patent is not subject to a licensing program, a reasonable royalty measures the damages. Reasonable royalty is defined as that amount that would have been agreed upon in a hypothetical negotiation between a willing patent owner and a willing potential user as of the date when the infringe-ment began. Because this is based on the assumption that the patent is valid, no dis-count is given for risk of patent invalidity, often a significant factor in lowering a negotiated royalty in the real world.

Court decisions applying an established royalty generally seek to determine whether sufficient evidence exists to show acquiescence to a royalty in similar cir-cumstances. Traditionally, little economic analysis has been used. In setting a rea-sonable royalty, the courts have inserted economic principles, but as a supplement to legal analyses rather than as an integrated approach to compensating a patent owner for lost patent profits. The courts look to several factors in setting a reasonable roy-alty, including: prior licenses under the patent;[16] industry custom on comparable licenses;[17] the relationship between the parties and the patent owner's licensing pol-icy;[18] the infringer's profits;[19] benefits over noninfringing alternatives;[20] and any col-lateral benefits.[21]

A strict application of these royalty measures not only allows the infringer to keep its economic profit, but also allows the infringer to keep a considerable portion of the patent profit. As discussed in Chapter 5, in negotiating a license to a patent, the patent profits are necessarily split between the licensor and the licensee. If either the patent owner or the licensee insisted on all the patent profits, the other party would have no incentive to enter into the license. When assessing patent damages, the royalty measure allows the infringer to keep those patent profits the willing licensee would have retained in a negotiation. Thus, the patent owner who cannot prove lost profits is often left with but a portion of the patent profits to which it is entitled, while the infringer is allowed to retain a portion of the patent profits. The offensiveness of allowing the infringer to retain this portion of the patent profit has not been lost on all courts. In fact, many courts simply increase the reasonable roy-alty award from a true "willing buyer–willing seller" negotiation to a higher royalty percentage to fully compensate the patent owner.[22]

## The Instant Camera Market

CASE STUDY

When George Eastman was 24, he became interested in photography. At that time, cameras were as big as microwave ovens and required a heavy tripod to support the weight. With the chemicals, glass plates, plate loader, water, and tent needed to process the photographs, a horse or mule was needed to move the equipment.

After three years of experiments, Eastman patented a new, dry-plate formula and a machine for preparing large numbers of the plates. In April 1880, Eastman started his company. He began to direct his experimentation to finding a lighter, more flexible support than glass. By 1885, Eastman had introduced a system of pho-tography that used roll holders. However, even after several improvements to this flexible, lightweight support, sales were disappointing.

◆

CASE

STUDY

◆

CONT.

Eastman's response was bold. Instead of targeting professionals only, he began consumer advertising to reach the general public. He coined the term, Kodak, which was to become one of the strongest, most recognized trademarks in the world. In 1888, he introduced the Kodak Camera under the tag line, "You push the button, we do the rest." This camera, priced at $25, came loaded with enough film for 100 exposures. After using up the film, the whole camera was returned to Eastman, who developed the film and inserted new film for $10.

Years later in 1944, Edward H. Land began working on "one-step photography." While vacationing in Santa Fe, New Mexico, Land photographed his daughter, who naively wondered why she had to wait to see the results. By 1947, he introduced a diffusion-transfer process in which the negative and positive were produced simultaneously. The first such camera was sold in the Jordan Marsh Department Store in Boston in November 1948. While the sale of this instant camera caused a sensation, users had to time and pull the film out of the camera, peel off and dispose of a protective chemical-covered paper backing, and apply a special coating to the final image. This instant camera also produced a sepia- or brown-colored photograph. In the early fifties, this sepia photograph was replaced by black and white film.

Dr. Land, however, pressed on. At his direction, in 1947 Howard G. Rogers began work on instant color film. By 1957 Polaroid had a prototype of an instant color film, which was introduced in 1963 under the name Polacolor. Polaroid issued at least three patents that related to the Polacolor film. All of these innovations, however, required the user to "pull and peel."

In 1972, Polaroid introduced the SX-70, an integrated camera that was a significant improvement in instant color photography. The SX-70 camera used a sleek folding design. More importantly, the film developed before the eyes of the user without any special handling. The SX-70 was so revolutionary that both Time and Life magazines featured the camera in cover stories.

The success of the instant camera business was not lost on Kodak. In early 1969, Kodak launched project PL-976; the goal was to introduce an instant camera by 1976. During the 1970s, Kodak investigated a variety of photographic chemistries. The goal of Project-129, an offshoot of Project-976, was to develop an instant color film similar to Polacolor and compatible with Polaroid cameras. The goal of Project-130, also an offshoot of Project-976, was to develop an integrated instant color system, using Kodak film in a Kodak camera.

Despite expenditures of $94 million, Kodak abandoned Project-129 shortly after Polaroid introduced the SX-70. Project-130 continued. By early 1972, Kodak had created an instant color camera model. Because of its shortcomings when compared to the SX-70, this camera was not introduced. In 1976, Kodak finally introduced an integral instant color camera. The cost to Kodak was enormous. Between late 1973 and mid-1975, between 1,300 and 1,400 employees were assigned to the instant camera project. A September 1973 memo drafted by Kodak's Development Committee stated that, "[d]evelopment should not be constrained by what an individual feels is potential patent infringement."[23]

In April 1976, Kodak introduced its instant camera in Canada. Days later, Polaroid sued Kodak for patent infringement. The lawsuit involved eleven patents. Six of the patents were directed towards the chemicals in the film and five were directed towards the mechanics of the camera. The oldest patent related to the Polacolor film design and seven of the patents related to the SX-70 system. The remaining two patents related to an alternative design to create a "dark room" in the camera that wasn't used in the SX-70. Dr. Land himself invented three of the patents, Rogers invented another three, and other Polaroid engineers invented the remaining patents.

The case was divided into two phases. The first phase was to determine whether Polaroid's patents were infringed. If so, the second phase would determine the damage award. Trial on the first phase occurred over nearly a five-month period some five years after the lawsuit was filed. The trial did not go well for Kodak. The court found Kodak infringed seven of the eleven patents and entered an injunction that put Kodak out of the instant camera business. By this time, Kodak had lost more than $600 million on its instant camera venture and was facing a damage award that many stock analysts estimated could be as high as $3 billion. Some were even predicting the bankruptcy and acquisition of Kodak by Polaroid to satisfy the damage award.

The damage phase occurred some eight years after infringement was found. This trial lasted 96 days. The goal of the damages award in patent cases is to place the patent owner in the position he would have enjoyed if the infringement had never happened. In this case, 186 witnesses testified "of what would have happened in a world that never existed," in the words of the judge.[24]

Polaroid argued that without Kodak, it would not have lowered prices and would have introduced new camera models in a slower, more deliberative manner to exploit manufacturing and marketing efficiencies. Therefore, according to Polaroid, Polaroid's sales would have been at a higher price and would have occurred later if not for Kodak. Polaroid also argued that Kodak trashed the instant camera market by introducing a low-priced model that consumers viewed as a gimmick. In effect, Polaroid was arguing that without Kodak it would have been able to raise prices without lowering demand. According to Polaroid's econometric model, Polaroid would have made an additional profit of more than $3.9 billion. Additionally, Polaroid argued that the infringement of the seven patents by Kodak was willful, thus requiring a punitive damages award of treble the actual damage, or more than $11 billion.

Kodak did not see it that way. Kodak argued that it had contributed to the expansion of the instant camera market and that, without Kodak, total sales would

⬥

CASE

STUDY

⬥

CONT.

have been considerably lower. According to Kodak's econometric model, the market would have been 75 percent smaller without Kodak, with the damage award based on this smaller market.

The court found Polaroid's argument overreached. It rejected Polaroid's claim that without Kodak it would have been able to raise prices without lowering demand. The court felt that either prices would have remained low to generate the same demand or increased prices would have lowered the demand. In the absence of a more restrained damage claim, the court found damages of more than $900 million. Also, despite the existence of the "smoking gun" memo advising researchers to ignore patents, the judge found the noninfringement analysis Kodak received from a New York patent law firm avoided willful infringement. Including the operating loss incurred before exiting the market, Kodak lost more than $1.5 billion in its effort to compete in the instant camera market.

And how did Wall Street respond to this historic damage award? Amazingly, after the award Polaroid's stock price fell more than 20 percent while Kodak's rose nearly 10 percent. Thus, the street clearly was expecting a much higher damage award and built that expectation into the stock prices of the two companies.

## Chapter 7

1. *Fitzgerald Publishing Co. v. Baylor Publishing Co.*, 807 F. 2d 1110 (2d Cir. 1986).

2. *Copyrights* Title 17, U.S. CODE, §412.

3. *Panduit Corp. v. Stahlin Bros. Fibre Works, Inc.*, 575 F. 2d 1152 (6th Cir. 1978); *Bio-Rad Laboratories, Inc. v. Nicolet Instruments Corp.*, 739 F. 2d 604 (Fed. Cir.), *cert. denied*, 469 U.S. 1038 (1984).

4. *State Industries, Inc. v. Mor-Flo Industries, Inc.* 883 F. 2d 1575 (Fed. Cir. 1989).

5. *Milgo Electronic Corp. v. United Business Communications, Inc.*, 623 F. 2d 645 (10th Cir.), *cert. denied*, 449 U.S. 1066 (1980).

6. *Manville Sales Corp. v. Paramount Systems Inc.*, 14 U.S.P.Q. 2d 1291 (E.D. Pa. 1989), *aff'd.*, 917 F. 2d 544 (Fed. Cir. 1990).

7. *Central Soya Co. v. Geo. A. Hormell & Co.*, 723 F. 2d 1573 (Fed. Cir. 1983).

8. *Smithkline Diagnostics, Inc. v. Helena Laboratories Corp.*, 12 U.S.P.Q. 2d 1375 (E.D. Tex. 1989), *aff'd.*, 926 F. 2d 1161 (Fed. Cir. 1991).

9. *Water Technologies Corp. v. Calco, Ltd.*, 850 F. 2d 665 (Fed. Cir.), *cert. denied*, 488 U.S. 968 (1988).

10. *Datascope Corp. v. SMEC, Inc.*, 678 F. Supp. 457 (D.N.J. 1988), *aff'd in part, rev'd in part*, 879 F. 2d 820 (Fed. Cir. 1989).

11. *Kaufman Co. v. Lantech, Inc.*, 926 F. 2d 1136, 1142 (Fed. Cir. 1991).

12. *Minnesota Mining & Manufacturing Co. v. Johnson & Johnson Orthopedics, Inc.*, 976 F. 2d 1559 (Fed. Cir. 1992).

13. *Brooktree Corp. v. Advanced Micro Devices, Inc.*, 977 F. 2d 1555 (Fed. Cir. 1992).

14. *Rite-Hite Corp. v. Kelley Co., Inc.*, 56 F. 3d 1538 (Fed. Cir. 1995).

15. *King Instruments Corp. v. Perego*, 65 F. 3d 941 (Fed. Cir. 1995).

16. *Studiengesellschaft Kohle, GmbH v. Dart Industries, Inc.*, 862 F. 2d 1564 (Fed. Cir. 1988).

17. *American Original Corp. v. Jenkins Food Corp.*, 774 F. 2d 459 (Fed. Cir. 1985).

18. *Smithkline Diagnostics, Inc. v. Helena Laboratories Corp.*, 926 F. 2d 11 61 (Fed. Cir. 1991).

19. *Trall v. Marlee Electronics Corp.*, 912 F. 2d 1443 (Fed. Cir. 1990).

20. *State Industries v. Mor-Flo Industries.*

21. *TWM Mfg. Co. v. Dura Corp.*, 789 F. 2d 895 (Fed. Cir.), *cert. denied*, 479 U.S. 852 (1986).

22. *Fromson v. Western Litho Plate & Supply Co.*, 853 F. 2d 1568 (Fed. Cir. 1988).

23. *Polaroid Corp. v. Eastman Kodak Co.*, 228 U.S.P.Q. 305, 308 (D. Mass 1985).

24. *Polaroid Corp. v. Eastman Kodak Co.*, 16 U.S.P.Q. 2d 1481, 1483 (D.Mass 1990).

## CHAPTER 8

# ACQUISITION

**The**

**End Game**

George, Mildred, and Chip's journey was about to end; it was cash-out time. About three months ago, George had realized that his company was at a crossroads. While the technology he had licensed in had improved the gargle-blaster speakers, it had not allowed him to extend his product line beyond speakers. And while sustained profitability was just around the corner, he realized that without significant additional investment in new products his vision of an initial public offering was a distant hope. He also realized that without significant investment, his company was in real danger of joining the living dead — profitable, but with little chance of further growth. He knew that if they could cash out now, while the profits were still growing, they would receive full value for their company.

He could sell out to an existing consumer electronics company and realize a healthy return; however, he believed they still had an opportunity for something greater. He had identified a potential strategic partner with an emerging technology that had a great synergistic potential when combined with the gargle-blaster technology. This emerging technology was for an improved audio amplification process that could provide studio quality sound from matchbox-sized amplifiers. Alone, this technology had the potential of revolutionizing the audio industry. With the gargle-blaster technology, it could well make existing audio technology obsolete, from automotive to theater applications.

Even though the progress of this technology was behind his gargle-blaster technology, both the potential and the amount of institutional funding behind this new technology left little doubt as to who was acquiring whom. If he was to sell the company for cash to a consumer electronics company, he would have great confidence in the value of what he would receive — cold, hard cash. However, this strategic merger was to be structured as a stock deal. Thus, George knew that he would need to do more due diligence into the emerging technology than they would into the already established gargle-blaster technology.

## Appropriate Depth

While acquisition intellectual property due diligence parallels startup due diligence in many respects, it also includes factors that are unique. In any type of acquisition, entrepreneurial managers should perform due diligence to a depth appropriate for the circumstances. The value of the intellectual property and the risk of conflict in commercializing the intellectual property are important factors in determining this depth. For example, the importance of environmental due diligence in acquiring even an expensive residential condominium pales in comparison to the importance of environmental due diligence in acquiring a gasoline station. Likewise, the importance of intellectual property due diligence in acquiring a generic commodity product line is less — although valuable trade-secret rights may be present — than in acquiring newly developed, high-technology consumer products.

Like any due diligence, decisions on the depth of intellectual property due diligence should be made in light of appropriate cost/benefit analysis. The size of the transaction and the importance of the intellectual property guide cost/benefit decisions on the intellectual property due diligence. A good guide is to estimate the proportion of the value of the transaction which is tied into the intellectual property — bearing in mind this is often a large portion of the goodwill of the transaction — and multiply this by the value of the transaction. This gives an estimate of the value of the intellectual property. Once this value is estimated, an appropriate depth of due diligence can be mapped out.

Like other technology due diligence, intellectual property due diligence in an acquisition entails three stages:

- ▶ Is the title to the intellectual property clean?
- ▶ Does exploitation of the intellectual property infringe any third party rights?
- ▶ What is the potential value of the intellectual property?

All, none, or some of these stages are appropriate depending on the nature of the transaction. In addition, because most intellectual property extends only within national boundaries, the applicable inquiries should be directed to each country where sufficient value in the intellectual property resides.

## Ensuring Clean Title

In stage one due diligence, ensuring that title to the intellectual property is clean depends on the type of intellectual property at issue. For patents and federally registered trademarks, a review of the appropriate governmental agency's records should be made to confirm ownership. In addition, the records should be checked to ensure that any fees have been paid to keep the intellectual property in effect. For trade secrets, copyrights, and common law trademarks, the development of these rights should be understood, with a view to ensuring that those involved have clearly assigned their rights to the target. Similarly, it should be confirmed that those involved with the creation of patents, copyrights, and trademarks properly assigned their rights to the target. Thus, review of employment agreements, consulting agreements, and the like should be made.

If a significant value — estimated in the same way as the value of intellectual property — resides in trade-secret rights, special issues arise. As described in detail in the Introduction, to be entitled to maintain information as trade secret, reasonable steps need to be made to maintain the information as confidential. Thus, steps taken by the target to maintain the information as confidential should be understood, including employment agreements, workplace security, and employee turnover. Special focus should be placed on the target's contracts with anyone exposed to these rights, such as suppliers, distributors, and customers.

The analysis of copyrights (including software) also presents special issues, as described in Chapter 4. If consultants were used, their agreements should be reviewed to ensure that the copyrights were assigned to the target. If the consultant had employees or used subcontractors, these same considerations should be given.

If value resides in trademarks, the diligence of the target in enforcing its rights should be understood. As described in Chapter 3, trademarks can be narrowed significantly if diligence is not exhibited in protecting trademarks. Any enforcement actions, such as cease and desist letters or lawsuits should be reviewed. Additionally, it is often helpful to conduct an independent survey of related uses of similar marks to understand the scope of protection surrounding a trademark. This is particularly significant if one of the synergies of the transaction consists of product or brand extensions.

If the target does not own the intellectual property, but rights have been obtained by license, an understanding of the licensed rights is essential. Initially, the barrier that such license provides can vary from an exclusive licensee (which is tantamount to ownership) to nonexclusive. The financial impact of any royalty payments should be understood as an additional cost-of-goods sold. The transferability of such rights, which can vary based on the legal form of the transaction, needs to be assessed and, if in doubt, may be an appropriate condition precedent to the close of the transaction. Finally, any limitations that are placed on the licensed rights, such as a limited field-of-use license, should be understood, particularly if one of the synergies of the transaction is in extending the intellectual property beyond the current exploitation. This applies as well to limits placed on intellectual property use by the target, such as the licensing-out of intellectual property.

## Third Party Rights

Beyond clear title to the intellectual property, if the nature of the transaction includes the introduction of new products, stage two due diligence focuses on whether the exploitation of the intellectual property could infringe on third party rights. For example, as explained in detail in chapters 2 and 6, the grant of a patent gives the patent owner the right to exclude others from making, using, or selling that which is within the scope of the patent. The patent grant does not give the patent owner an affirmative right to commercialize the technology if it infringes other third party rights. The degree of risk of a third party owning a blocking patent can vary significantly with the circumstances of the intellectual property.

Stage Two Due Diligence

For example, acquiring patents to a hot new technology that has never been commercially exploited carries a much higher risk than a product line sold for years without incurring any challenges. Unlike trademarks, the obligation of patent owners to enforce their rights is not absolute; sales for a short period of time can lull the acquirer into a false sense of security. For example, the unchallenged threat of sales by an underfunded startup may be challenged if acquired by a well-funded adversary.

Like patents, copyrights should be understood to ensure that the copyrighted work is not subordinate. As fully explained in Chapter 4, derivative works, joint works, and other forms of copyrighted material present issues of the right of the owner to exploit the copyrighted work.

## Potential Value

Finally, in stage three due diligence the potential value of the intellectual property should be explored with the focus on the availability of economic substitute products. While much of this analysis is within the role of the marketing and financial disciplines, the patent attorney must help these professionals understand the scope of the rights. In addition to the acquisition of intellectual property, this type of stage three due diligence is particularly applicable to licensing opportunities.

Stage Three Due Diligence

The scope of patents available to the new technology should be understood so that the level of competition from economic substitute products can be considered. As described in Chapter 2, to access the scope of patents, the correspondence between the patent applicant and the patent office should be reviewed to understand any "concessions" made by the applicant in negotiating the issuance of the patent. Additionally, the state of the technological art over which the patent was allowed should be surveyed to understand the significance of the technological innovation.

The techniques of patent charting described in detail in Chapter 6 represent a particularly efficient way for entrepreneurial managers to gain an intuitive understanding of these issues.

The strength of any trademarks should be explored. As described in Chapter 3, the category into which the trademark fits should be determined. If the term is descriptive and has become protectable through the acquisition of secondary meaning, the sales and advertising expenditures should be reviewed to assess the strength of the trademark. Additionally, an independent survey of related uses of similar marks can help define the scope of protection surrounding a trademark.

As with any type of due diligence, entrepreneurial managers understand that no amount of depth can completely eliminate risk. For example, due to the confidential nature of many applications, applications that may issue as patents in the future cannot be reviewed. Like all due diligence, the art of intellectual property due diligence is in properly assessing the cost/benefit tradeoffs on a case-by-case basis.

## Postscript

As he admired the view on the Caribbean vacation he and Mildred took to celebrate the "sale" of Marvin Enterprises, George contemplated the future. While Marvin Enterprises had not made them the next Bill Gates — they had rented, not purchased a townhouse near the beach — George, Mildred, and Chip Norton had made out well in the merger of their company. And with new management at the helm of the combined ship, George and Mildred could go on to new things. Mildred had already made it clear what she wanted to do — she planned on using some of the financial freedom the Marvins had gained to give something back to the community. Chip, exhausted from his experience, planned on taking some time off and then getting an engineering job back "in the real corporate world," as he put it.

George likewise wanted some time off, but was already getting restless. Prior to his vacation, George had lunch with Ted, his old boss at the consumer electronic company, who had recently been promoted. Ted had made a pitch for George to return and run his old division, which was now part of the group for which Ted was responsible. George was confident that with his experience at Marvin Enterprises he could juice up the division with entrepreneurial management; and like Chip, the idea of returning to the stability of the "real corporate world" held some attraction.

George was also intrigued by a conversation he had had with a venture capitalist friend some weeks before the sale of Marvin Enterprises. This VC told George about a new electronics invention that had some fascinating potential. It seemed as though the invention had been made by someone like Chip who, although a technical genius, clearly had his limitations in strategically thinking about how to commercialize the technology. George relished the idea of applying his experience to avoid the mistakes he had made in commercializing his gargle-blaster speakers. However, he was not sure if he or Mildred were ready for the time and energy commitment that would be required for another startup situation. As he sipped his Jamaican beer, he told Mildred, "Well, there's no harm in talking to my VC buddy, just to see what's been going on." As Mildred saw the fire in his eyes, she understood better than George that he had the startup bug in his blood.

# PATENT APPLICATION

Typically, to draft and file a patent application in the U.S. Patent Office costs about $5,000–$8,000. From the time a technical disclosure is received from an inventor, an attorney will need approximately two to four weeks to prepare an initial draft for review by the inventor. Depending on the extent of the inventor's comments and changes, the application should be ready to file in the U.S. Patent Office in another one to three weeks.

## The Technical Disclosure

A patent application is a complex document having both technical and legal requirements. The technical requirements of a patent application include a detailed technical description of the invention. It is not unlike an article drafted for a technical journal and involves a corresponding time commitment from the inventors in describing the invention.

The description in a patent must be sufficient to enable a fictional person "skilled in the art" to replicate the invention. As a tradeoff for the governmental grant of the limited exclusivity of a patent, full disclosure about the invention must be provided. In practice, this information regarding the invention cannot be held back, but must describe in detail the "best mode" or the best-known way of practicing the invention. Finally, the description should particularly point out what is different and better about the invention to show that the invention would not have been obvious to the fictional person "skilled in the art."

To meet these requirements, detailed discussion should address several areas:

1. Background of the Invention.

    a. Describe existing devices or processes already on the market against which the commercial implementation of this invention will compete. Discuss the disadvantages of these previous devices or processes and how the present device or process is superior.

    b. Include additional information needed to give a complete description regarding the state of the technical field or alternative approaches in the field. Also, provide copies of all information that may be relevant to the invention (for example, prior patents, articles, and product literature).

2. Detailed Description of a Preferred Embodiment.

    a. If the invention is physical (for example, mechanical or electrical), provide detailed drawings (CAD drawings or blueprints, if possible) of the device from several different views. If alternative designs are contemplated which have similar advantages, provide drawings of each alternative design, and if possible, a view of the device as a perspective either alone or in its intended environment.

    b. If the invention is not physical (for example, chemical or biochemical), submit all notebook pages regarding the development of the invention, including charts, experimental results, reactions, and chemical structures.

    c. If the invention relates to physics, a detailed description of any applicable formulas is needed, including how such formulas were derived.

    d. If the invention relates to software, include detailed, accurate, and comprehensive flow charts of the system's logic. In addition, provide a description of the logic flow of the system. If appropriate, also include schematic architectural overview diagrams of the interface of the components of the system as well as the preferred hardware on which the software will be run.

    e. Each part in each drawing provided must be named with particularity, including a brief description of the function or purpose of each part (for example, "Element D1 is a diode which acts to block reverse current flow"). If a group of parts within the device function as a sub-unit, the group of parts should be named and their cooperative function described (for example, "Diode elements D5–D8 together make up full wave bridge rectifier which acts to provide full wave rectification of the power source.").

If the invention is not physical, include a complete discussion regarding the development of the invention.

## Prosecution

After the application is filed in the U.S. Patent Office, the process of negotiating, or prosecuting the patent begins. It is particularly difficult to estimate the cost or time frame for this stage. This is because, as with any negotiation, much depends on the attitude of the other party in the negotiation. The usual first step is for the examiner at the patent office to issue an "office action" explaining the examiner's position. This is likely to occur from three to twelve months after the application is filed. As with any negotiation, more than 90 percent of the time the examiner rejects the opening offer. A response is then filed. This is typically a written response, although a face-to-face meeting or a conference call can be arranged with the examiner. The face-to-face meeting can be helpful when the nature of the invention makes describing it on paper difficult.

Responses to and from the examiner can go on indefinitely, but typically occur two to three times. Each round costs about $1,500–$3,000 in legal fees and takes about three to six months to occur. Thus, the average pendancy of the application is about two to three years. At the conclusion of the process, an adverse decision by the examiner can be appealed within the patent office to a board of three senior examiners and even beyond that, to the Federal Circuit.

In addition to meeting face-to-face with the examiner, "objective" evidence of patentability can be submitted. This can include, for example, evidence of the commercial success of the patented technology in the form of sales figures, or a long-felt need for the technology in the form of laudatory articles. This evidence is submitted in the form of affidavit testimony, which the attorney drafts and files. While adding about $2,000–$4,000 to the cost, this type of evidence can be persuasive.

The least expensive route is to simply respond in writing to the office actions, with no appeal of a decision. If the patent is rejected, the examiner has not been reasonable, and a good chance of overturning the examiner on appeal exists, the examiner can be appealed by simply filing an appeal brief and foregoing an oral hearing. This adds about $2,000–$4,000 to the cost. An oral hearing adds another $2,000–$4,000. Likewise, a face-to-face meeting with the examiner adds a similar amount to the cost. The patent issues about three to four months after completion of the prosecution, with an additional cost of about $1,500.

Thus, the total costs range from as little as $8,000 — if an examiner is cooperative, a face-to-face meeting is not required, no subjective evidence is developed and submitted to the examiner, and an appeal is not necessary — to $20,000 or more in the most expensive case scenario. From a strategic perspective, it often becomes clear during the process that little or no return will be gained on many of these steps such as, for example, the face-to-face meeting.

To keep a patent in force, periodic payments referred to as "maintenance fees" must be made. Maintenance fees for a patent are required at $3\frac{1}{2}$ years, $7\frac{1}{2}$ years and $11\frac{1}{2}$ years. Although fees change periodically, the approximate amounts of these fees are $1,000, $2,000, and $3,200 for large corporations and $525, $1,000, and $1,600 for individuals, respectively.

## Foreign Patents

The costs for filing in foreign countries vary considerably based on many factors, including the fees due to the government, the number of countries chosen in a regional application, the cost of any required translations, the complexity of the applications, and exchange rates. The approximate costs for some of the most frequently chosen routes are:

| | |
|---|---|
| PCT | $2,500–$3,500 |
| EPO | $8,000–$15,000 |
| United Kingdom | $2,500–$3,500 |
| France | $3,500–$5,000 |
| Germany | $3,500–$5,000 |
| Canada | $2,000–$3,000 |
| Japan | $15,000–$25,000 |
| Australia | $2,500–$3,500 |

For each country or regional application, additional expenditures are necessary to examine, prosecute, issue, and maintain the patent. As with the cost of prosecuting a patent in the United States, the cost of prosecuting the patent in each country could vary greatly depending on the attitude of the individual examiner to whom the application is assigned.

# TRADEMARK APPLICATION

The

Filing

Process

Unlike patents, filing a trademark application in the U.S. Trademark Office is relatively inexpensive, about $500–$1,000. After the application is filed the process of prosecuting the trademark begins. The usual first step is for the examining attorney at the trademark office to issue an office action explaining his or her position. This is likely to occur from three to six months after the application is filed. Unlike the expected response in patent prosecution, often this office action contains formal objections that can be easily disposed of to obtain registration of the trademark.

However, three substantive actions can occur. Initially, the examining attorney actually categorizes the trademark in one of the categories described in Chapter 3: generic, descriptive, suggestive, or arbitrary. If the examining attorney believes the mark is generic or descriptive, the application will be rejected. To overcome this rejection, the applicant must convince the examining attorney (or the Appeals Board) that the mark is suggestive.

The examining attorney also performs a search for conflicting marks. If the examining attorney believes use of the mark is likely to cause confusion with a pre-existing registration, the application will be rejected. To overcome this rejection, the applicant must convince the examining attorney (or the Appeals Board) that no likelihood of confusion exists.

Finally, the examining attorney can object to the scope or breadth of the description of the goods or services. Obviously, the broader the description of the goods or services, the better for the trademark owner. Thus, compromise as to the breadth of the description occurs. This is often done when distinguishing any prior registrations cited by the examiner.

These responses are typically made in the form of a written response, although a conference call can be arranged with the examining attorney, particularly when formal issues need to be resolved. Responses to and from the examining attorney can go on indefinitely, but typically two to three times. Each round costs about $500–$1,500 in legal fees, and typically takes three to six months to occur. Thus, the application is pending on average about one to two years. At the conclusion of the process, an adverse decision by the examiner can be appealed within the trademark office to a board of three senior examiners and even beyond that to the Federal Circuit.

After acceptance of the trademark registration, it is published in an official government publication. The purpose of this publication is to give notice to any prior trademark owners who believe the registration of the trademark conflicts with their rights. If a prior trademark owner believes the registration of the trademark conflicts with their rights, they can adjudicate this issue in an administrative lawsuit referred to as an "opposition." A similar proceeding called a "cancellation" is available to cancel registration of a trademark if a prior trademark owner believes the registration of the trademark conflicts with their rights. While typically not as expensive as a regular lawsuit, an opposition or cancellation proceeding can run in the tens and even hundreds of thousands of dollars.

Thus, the total costs may be as little as $1,000 if an examining attorney is cooperative, an appeal is not necessary, and no opposition is filed.

# COPYRIGHT APPLICATION

Procuring a copyright is extremely affordable. While copyright notice is not required, notice achieves the business goal of informing potential infringers that the copyright owner considers the work to be a valuable property that will be defended and makes certain damages available. Given the cost of placing copyright notices on copyrightable materials, nearly anything a company disseminates should include the simple notice: "© [year of creation], [owner's name]" or "Copyright [year of creation], [owner's name]."

Likewise, the most significant reasons for actually registering the copyrighted work at the copyright office are to demonstrate to potential infringers the seriousness with which the owners view their rights, make certain damages available, and conclusively evidence the date of creation. Before bringing suit for copyright infringement, the work must be registered.

Unlike patents, a copyright application in the U.S. Copyright Office undergoes no substantive examination. Thus, the only cost of registering a copyright is the filing fee of about $500 and the time needed to fill out a (relatively) simple form. Thus, for works in which the value resides in the expression of the idea, such as sculptures, books, plays, and, perhaps, widely-disseminated software, registration should be considered. However, registration on all copyrightable works a company generates, such as brochures, advertising copy, marketing materials, and label designs can be expensive. Since the point of enforcing copyrights on these materials is often to stop a knock-off competitor, companies often wait to register such materials until a lawsuit is anticipated.

# GLOSSARY

**absolute novelty.** Under an absolute novelty system, many forms of disclosure to third parties and many types of commercial activity, if occurring prior to the filing date of the patent application, act to bar issuance of a valid patent. Absolute novelty is contrasted with the patent system in the United States, in which a twelve month "grace period" is provided.

**abstract.** The part of the patent that contains a brief summary of the disclosure of the invention.

**algorithm.** A term that, because of its dual meaning, has caused a great deal of confusion in the evolution of the application of patents to software innovations. A mathematical algorithm is a procedure for solving a given mathematical problem and is considered unpatentable as a law of nature. This is distinguished from a computer algorithm, which defines a step-by-step procedure for accomplishing a given result in a computer, and is considered patentable subject matter.

**anticipation.** In order for an invention to be patentable, it must be new or different from the existing body of technological information. If a single reference in the existing body of technological information reveals every requirement set forth in a claim, that reference is said to "anticipate" the invention.[1]

**apparatus claim.** Defines the invention as a structure. This type of claim is contrasted with a method claim, which defines the invention by a series of steps to be followed in performing a process.

**arbitrary mark.** An arbitrary brand name neither suggests nor describes any quality or characteristic of the particular good or service. Arbitrary marks are strong trademarks but can require a significant investment of marketing resources to develop consumer recognition.

**barrier to entry.** Factors that prevent potential competitors from entering a market, such as government rules or patents.

**best mode.** The best form or embodiment of an invention at the time a patent application is filed; a requirement of the patent specification.[2]

**brand name.** A marketing term that generally means the same thing as a trademark.

**broadening reissue.** A Reissue Application must be filed within two years of the grant date of a patent when the patent claims, erroneously, less than the patent has a right to claim. This error is corrected by reissuing a broader patent.

**business methods patents.** A category of patentable subject matter for less-traditional patentable technology that arose from the 1999 court decision of *State Street v. Signature*.[3]

**cease and desist letter.** A letter informing a competitor of the existence of intellectual property rights, asserting that those rights are being infringed, and demanding that the infringing activity stop.

**claim.** That part of a patent that maps out or defines the subject matter that is the exclusive property of the patentee for the duration of the patent.

**coined mark.** A word invented for the purpose of serving as a trademark. Coined marks are the strongest trademarks but can require a significant investment of marketing resources to develop consumer recognition.

**commercial success.** Marketplace evidence of patentability that examines the commercial success of a product that is attributable to the importance of the invention.

**compilation.** A copyrightable work consisting of an assembly of preexisting material.

**conception.** The first step in the invention process in which the inventor unambiguously has a definite perception of the complete and operative invention.[4] In priority contests under the "first to invent" system of the United States, conception can define the date of invention.

**continuation application.** A second patent application for the same invention by the same inventor and containing the same description as the first patent application.[5] This procedure is often used to make additional arguments on the merits to the patent office after a final rejection.

continuation-in-part application (C-I-P). A second application which adds additional information not contained in the disclosure of the first application.[6] The continuation-in-part application is best viewed as a supplemental filing if further inventions related to the technology are made or if the commercial form of the technology evolves in an unexpected direction.

contributory infringement. Indirect infringement of intellectual property rights in which the defendant contributes to another party's direct infringement of such rights.

convoy damages. A measure of damages in patent infringement cases, including sales of nonpatented complementary products that would have been sold by the patent owner if the infringing products had not been sold.[7]

copyright. A right owned by an author of a work to exclude others who have had access to the work from creating a substantially similar work. Protection is confined to the expression of an idea, but does not cover the idea itself.

critical date. The date one year prior to filing a U.S. patent application that establishes the time under which an inventor's activities are judged to determine whether the invention was in public use or offered for sale, thus invalidating the patent.

dependent claim. Claims can be written in either independent or dependent format. A dependent claim refers back to a previous claim, incorporates all of the requirements in the previous claim, and either adds or more specifically defines an existing requirement. Dependent claims generally define a narrow scope of a patent, but are more difficult to invalidate.

derivative work. A copyrightable work that changes, condenses, or embellishes a preexisting work in some way.

descriptive. A term that, when used as a brand name for goods or service, describes a quality or characteristic of the goods or services. A descriptive term is not entitled to trademark status until sufficient consumer connection between the descriptive term and the goods and services has been established, referred to as secondary meaning.

design around. The process of designing a product in order to compete against a patented product but avoid infringing that patent.

design patent. An exclusive grant in a novel, nonobvious, and ornamental industrial design.

dilution. A form of infringement of a trademark in which the infringing use does not cause a likelihood of confusion but tarnishes the image of a strong trademark.[8]

divisional application. A second application on a different invention which is disclosed and thus carved out of a first pending application.[9] A divisional application is usually filed after a "restriction requirement" in which the patent office determines that the claims defined more than one invention and requires the applicant to restrict the application to only one invention. Although directed at a second invention, a divisional application discloses only the information contained in the first application.

**doctrine of equivalents.** A doctrine of claim interpretation under which, even if the actual language of the claim does not literally read on a device, if an equivalent of that element is present in the device, the device can infringe the claim.[10] The doctrine of equivalents focuses on two inquiries: for chemical cases, the focus is the interchangeability of the elements; for mechanical cases, the focus is whether the element performs substantially the same function in substantially the same way to accomplish the same result as the patented requirement. For electrical and software cases, both inquiries can apply.

**economic barrier.** Characteristics of a given market niche industry that make it difficult for new competitors to enter. These barriers can include, for example, reduction in manufacturing cost per unit realized through operational efficiencies, high capital investment requirements, government regulations, and intellectual property rights.

**enablement.** The requirement that a patent must give a sufficiently clear technical description of the invention to enable a hypothetical person having ordinary skill in the art to replicate the invention without undue experimentation.[11]

**environmental change.** A change in some aspect of the environment in which a business operates that usually necessitates a change in the business' strategy.

**experimental use.** Exception to the on-sale and public use bars to patent validity. If an invention is disclosed prior to the critical date, but the disclosure had an experimental purpose necessary to finalize the invention, the patent is still valid.[12]

**failure of others.** Marketplace evidence of patentability under which the attempts and failures of others to solve a technological problem is evidence that the solution of such a technological problem is patentable.

**fair use.** A defense against copyright infringement that essentially admits access and substantial similarity to the infringed work, but relies on public policy that some forms of copying are acceptable. Fair use is based on factors such as the commercial versus educational aspects of the copied use, the degree of expression encompassed in the copied use, the amount and importance of the copied use, and the economic impact of the use on the market for the copyrighted work.

**family of marks.** Refers to the creation, by a common owner, of a group of trademarks having a common element that distinguishes them as related. Use of a family of marks can enhance the scope of protection of each individual trademark.

**field of use.** A way to carve up patent rights into different types of applications by defining and licensing to different entities different categories of commercial exploitation encompassed by the scope of the patent.

**file wrapper.** Literally comes from the folder in which the correspondence to and from the patent applicant are kept at the U.S. Patent Office. It is also known as the "prosecution history."

**first to file.** A patent system in which the applicant who first files the application at a patent office is awarded ownership of the patent. This is distinguished from the "first to invent" system of the United States.

**first to invent.** A patent system in which the applicant who first invented the patentable subject matter is awarded ownership of the patent. An administrative lawsuit referred to as an "interference" is used to determine who first invented. This is distinguished from the "first to file" systems used outside the United States.

**forum shopping.** The legal strategy of filing a lawsuit in a jurisdiction based on the perceived biases of that jurisdiction rather than the convenience of the location.

**functional claim language.** The claim-drafting strategy that uses descriptions of function instead of structure. Usually done in "means plus function" format. Once favored, recent court decisions tend to give functional language a narrow interpretation.

**generic term.** A term that has become so associated with a class of goods and services that it is incapable of achieving trademark status.

**genericide.** When brand names become so ingrained in the consuming public's subconscious that they become generic and no longer merit trademark status.

**geographic.** Geographic marks relating to the geographic origin of goods or services are considered to be descriptive, thus entitled to trademark protection only if the mark has developed secondary meaning.

**goodwill.** The value of a business that extends beyond the value of the hard assets owned by the business. Goodwill reflects the potential of a business to earn future profits and can consist in large part of intellectual property.

**grace period.** The one-year period given to an inventor after a public disclosure or commercial sales activity within which the inventor can file for an application for a U.S. patent. If this one-year period passes without a patent application being filed, the public disclosure or commercial sales activity itself becomes part of the "prior art" in the public domain, effectively barring the grant of a patent on the innovation. This grace period contrasts with the patent systems in most countries outside the United States where "absolute novelty" is required.

**independent claim.** Claims can be written in either independent or dependent format. An independent claim contains all of the claim requirements in one claim. Independent claims generally define the broadest scope of a patent, but are easier to invalidate.

**inequitable conduct.** When an applicant obtained a patent because they did not disclose to the patent office all of the information about the invention of which they were aware, the applicant is said to have conducted inequitable conduct and the patent cannot be enforced.

**information disclosure statement.** The mechanism by which all of the relevant prior art of which the applicant is aware is conveyed to the patent office.

**intent-to-use trademark application.** An optional procedure for filing for federal registration of a trademark prior to actual commercial use of that trademark.

**interference.** An administrative lawsuit in the patent and trademark offices used to determine which of two inventors was the first to invent a patentable invention or which of two trademark owners was the first to use a trademark.[13]

**invention.** The creation of a new technical idea, including the physical means to accomplish or embody the idea. This is distinguished from a "patentable invention," which is an invention that meets the criteria of patentability.

**inventive process.** The process by which a patentable invention comes into being. In order to support a date of invention, the invention process typically begins with conception, ends with reduction to practice, and is interceded by due diligence in completing the invention.

**inventor.** One who contributes to the solution of a problem that an invention solves.

**Jepson claim.** A format of a claim in which the old elements of the combination are set forth first in the preamble, and the main body of the claim sets forth the new elements of the invention.[14]

**know-how.** Knowledge that allows the holder to better accomplish a particular task. When know-how is outside the public domain and reasonable efforts are made to preserve confidentiality, it is a trade secret and protectable under the law.

**likelihood of confusion.** This is the legal standard applied to determine whether a trademark is infringed. Whether a likelihood of confusion exists is typically based on factors such as the strength of the mark, the degree of similarity between the conflicting marks, proximity of the goods or services, the sophistication of buyers, and any objective evidence such as actual confusion or proof of bad faith in choosing the mark.

**literal infringement.** Infringement of a patent when each and every limitation of a claim is found in an accused product or process. Typically, the inclusion of further elements in the product or process does not negate infringement.

**lost profits.** This is the measure of damage used to determine reimbursement to the intellectual property holder for the profits lost as a result of the infringing activity. Lost profits are not related to profits made by the infringer, but to the profits a patent owner would have made without the infringement. They are calculated using a broad range of economic phenomena.

**market share theory.** A patent damages theory under which the patent owner recovers lost sales based on that portion of the infringer's sales that corresponds to the patent owner's market share.[15]

**mask work.** The design of a semiconductor chip, which is protected under the Semiconductor Chip Protection Act (SCPA).[16]

**means-plus-function claim.** A strategy of defining the limitation of a claim by using functional claim language instead of the structure to describe what must be performed in an infringing device to infringe the claim.

**method claim.** A method claim defines the invention by a series of steps to be followed in performing a process. This type of claim is contrasted with an apparatus claim, which defines the invention as a structure.

**mutually blocking patents.** The situation that occurs when the scope of a preexisting patent from a prior invention encompasses the commercial embodiment of a subsequent invention. The owner of the prior patent can preclude the owner of the later patent from commercializing the improved technology; likewise, the owner of the later patent can preclude the owner of the prior patent from commercializing the prior invention in the form of the improvement that is encompassed by the later patent, even though this also is encompassed by the prior patent.[17]

**net present value.** The present value of an investment's future cash-flow discounted at an appropriate rate based on the risk of the investment and minus the initial investment.

**nonobviousness.** *See* obviousness.

**novelty.** In order for an invention to be patentable, it must be new or different from the existing body of technological information. If a single reference in the existing body of technological information reveals every requirement set forth in a claim, that claim is said to lack "novelty."[18]

**objective evidence.** Evidence of the actual marketplace reaction to an invention from which it logically follows that an invention was not obvious, such as commercial success, a long-felt need, unexpected results, failure of others, industry acquiescence, and favorable comments from objective sources, such as the trade press or even an accused infringer.

**obviousness.** For an invention to be patentable, it must be new or different from the existing body of technological information. Even if a single reference in the existing body of technological information does not reveal every requirement set forth in a claim, if the invention could be readily deduced by a hypothetical person of ordinary skill in the art, the claim is said to be "obvious."[19]

**on-sale bar.** Prohibitor of a patent on an invention that has been on sale, subject to certain commercial activity, more than one year before filing the application.[20]

**opportunity cost.** A decision to produce or consume a product involves giving up another product. The opportunity cost of a resource is measured by the value of the next-best alternative foregone in the pursuit of an activity.

**opposition.** An administrative lawsuit in which evidence and arguments are presented to persuade the patent or trademark office not to issue a patent or trademark. In the United States, a third party cannot challenge the issuance of a patent but can challenge the issuance of a trademark.

**paper patent.** A patent whose technology has not been built. Once considered a defense to patent infringement, there is no requirement under the law that the subject of a patent must have been built.

**parent application.** An earlier application on which a later application is based.

**Patent Cooperation Treaty.** The international treaty that established processes to prevent the necessity of filing patent applications simultaneously in multiple jurisdictions.

**patent flooding.** A strategy of obtaining a series of narrow patents on closely related embodiments of a technology in the hope of gaining a broad scope of exclusivity.

**patent marking.** The requirement to label products made in accordance with a patent that precludes certain limitations of a damage award under a defense of lack-of-notice by an infringer.

**Patent Pending.** The marking put on products to indicate that a patent application has been filed on technology embodied in the product.

**patentable invention.** An invention that meets the criteria of patentability: (1) patentable subject matter and (2) an inventive step over the existing body of technological information.

**pioneer patent.** A patent that covers technology that makes a significant advance over the technological state of the art. Pioneer patents are entitled to a broad interpretation under the doctrine of equivalents.[21]

**price taker.** A seller who must take the price determined by the forces of supply and demand on the market as a whole. Applies to a perfectly competitive market where perfect substitute products are sold.

**prior art.** The body of technological know-how against which a patent application is judged to determine whether it is patentable.

**prosecution.** Process of negotiating the grant of a patent or the registration of a trademark with the U.S. Patent and Trademark Office.

**prosecution history.** *See* file wrapper.

**prosecution history estoppel.** A limitation on the doctrine of equivalents, under which comments and concessions made by the patent applicant to the patent office in arguing for the grant of the patent can narrow the scope of equivalents.[22]

**provisional application.** An inventor can use this procedure to file a technical disclosure of the invention in order to create a record at the patent office of the state of the invention as of the filing date.

**public domain.** The status of something originally entitled to intellectual property protection, but for which the protection has expired, making it freely duplicable by anyone.

**public-use bar.** The public-use bar prohibits a patent on an invention that was publically disclosed more than one year before the application was filed.[23]

**read on.** The first stage in determining if a claim is infringed, which entails determining whether the description contained in the claim describes the device. If each requirement of a claim describes the device under scrutiny, the claim is said to read on the device and the claim is infringed.[24]

**reasonable royalty.** The floor of damages for patent infringement that awards the amount that would have been agreed upon in a hypothetical negotiation between a willing patent license owner and a willing licensee as of the date when the infringement began. This is often used when the patent owner does not commercially exploit the patented technology. Because it is based on the assumption that the patent is valid, no discount is given for risk of patent invalidity — often a significant factor in lowering a negotiated royalty in the real world.

**reduction to practice.** The final step in the inventive process which consists of the completion of the invention. If an actual working model has not been made, under the law, the act of filing a patent application is considered a constructive reduction to practice. Reduction to practice is an important concept in determining who among simultaneous developers has priority rights to an invention.

**reexamination.** A procedure in the patent office in which the validity of a patent can be reviewed based on information not originally considered in granting the patent.

**reference.** A source of prior art. This can include patents, books, journal articles, abstracts, advertisements, promotional literature, and other publications; and public disclosure or commercial activity occurring more than one year before the filing of the application.

**reissue application.** A reissue procedure involves a regranting by the patent office in order to correct a patent that is wholly inoperative or invalid.[25] Most significantly, if initiated within two years of the grant of a patent, the error of claiming less than the patent applicant had a right to claim can be corrected, resulting in a broader patent being reissued.

**restriction requirement.** A demand filed when the patent office takes the position that an application covers more than one invention,[26] and typically results in the applicant filing a divisional application.

**reverse doctrine of equivalents.** A corollary to the doctrine of equivalents under which: even when an accused device appears to literally infringe a patent, if the device is so far changed that it performs the function in a substantially different way, the device will not infringe.[27]

**reverse engineering.** A process of tearing apart a publicly available product to understand the technology incorporated in that product.

**SCPA.** The Semiconductor Chip Protection Act provides an exclusive right (a hybrid of patent and copyright) for ten years to reproduce the design of a semiconductor chip, known as a mask work.[28]

**secondary meaning.** The perception by consumers of a descriptive term as a trademark rather than as a descriptor for the goods; necessary for a descriptive term to be protectable as a trademark.

**service mark.** A word, slogan, design, picture, or any other symbol used to identify and distinguish services as opposed to goods.

**shrink-wrap license.** A type of copyright license (primarily for software) that attempts to bind a purchaser despite the lack of an executed agreement.

**skilled in the art.** The hypothetical standard by which the patentability of a technological development is judged. To be patentable, the invention must not have been obvious to the fictional person "skilled in the art." An example of such a person might be "a person with a masters in electrical engineering with at least five years experience in the field."

**specification.** That part of the patent in which the inventor specifies, describes, and discloses the invention in detail. The specification must satisfy the "enablement" and "best mode" requirements. The specification also is used to interpret claims.

**statutory bar.** Material that is included in the existing state of technology (including the inventor's own material) against which the patentability of an invention is judged when it was in existence more than twelve months before the date of application for a patent.[29]

**statutory damages.** A damage measure in copyright cases when damages are difficult to prove. For each copyrighted work infringed, damages range from $500 to $20,000 depending on factors such as "lost revenue" of the copyright owner and "expense saved and profits reaped" by the infringer.[30] Availability of statutory damages is contingent on registration of the copyright work upon creation.[31]

**step-plus-function claim.** A strategy of defining the limitations of a claim by using a series of steps instead of structure to describe what must be performed in an infringing device to infringe the claim. *See also* method claim.

**suggestive words.** Words used as brand names that "require imagination, thought, and perception to reach a conclusion about the nature of the goods."[32] Suggestive words are capable of acting as trademarks from the inception of their use.

**synergies.** Economic efficiencies that are not possible to achieve unilaterally, but which result from the integration of two entities' assets.

**term of patent.** A patent holder can prevent others from making, using, selling or offering to sell that which is covered by the patent for a term starting when the patent issues and ending 20 years from filing date of the application.[33]

**trade dress.** The impression given by the product and packaging as a whole which is protectable under the trademark laws.[34]

**trade name.** Symbol used to identify and distinguish a business entity from other business entities. Distinguished from trademarks and service marks, which identify a product or service.

**trade secret.** Information that is subject to reasonable efforts to preserve confidentiality and that gives the holder a competitive advantage.

**trademark.** "... any word, name, symbol or device or any combination thereof adopted and used by a manufacturer or merchant to identify his goods and distinguish them from those manufactured or sold by others."[35]

**unfair competition.** A category of intellectual property that encompasses the laws of trademarks, trade dress, false advertising, misappropriation of trade secretes, dilution, trade disparagement, and trade libel.

**utility.** The requirement of a patent that the invention have a useful function. Utility is radically different from commercial viability. In most areas of technology, it is only necessary for some minimal level of usefulness to be present.

**utility model.** An additional category of patent protection offered in many countries outside the United States which neither requires the same degree of nonobviousness nor extends the same scope of protection as regular patents.

**willful infringement.** Conduct under which an infringer of an intellectual property right has no good-faith basis for the behavior, thus may be exposed to punitive damages.

**work-for-hire.** A copyrightable work prepared by an employee or a consultant in certain defined categories where the copyright is vested in the employer from the moment of conception. A work-for-hire must fit into one of the following categories: (A) works prepared by an employee within the scope of his or her employments or (B) works that are specifically commissioned under a written agreement, provided the work is within one of nine categories: (1) contributions to collective works; (2) parts of motion picture or audio-visual aids; (3) translations; (4) supplemental works (for example, forewords); (5) compilations; (6) instructional texts; (7) tests; (8) test answers; and (9) atlases.[36]

## Endnotes

1. *Patents*, Title 35, U.S. CODE, §102.

2. Ibid., §112.

3. *State Street Bank and Trust Co. v. Signature Financial Group, Inc.*, 149 F. 3d 1368 (Fed. Cir. 1999).

4. *Coleman v. Dines*, 754 F. 2d 353, 359 (Fed. Cir. 1985).

5. *Patents*, Title 35, §120.

6. Ibid.

7. *Rite-Hite Corp. v. Kelley Co., Inc.*, 56 F. 3d 1538 (Fed. Cir. 1995); *King Instruments Corp. v. Perego*, 65 F. 3d 941 (Fed. Cir. 1995).

8. *Trademarks*, Title 15, U.S. CODE, §1125(c).

9. *Patents*, Title 35, §121.

10. *Warner-Jenkinson Co., Inc. v. Hilton Davis Chemical Co.*, 520 U.S. 17 (1997).

11. *Patents*, Title 35, §112.

12. *City of Elizabeth v. American Nicholson Pavement Co.*, 97 U.S. 126 (1878).

13. *Patents*, Title 35, §135.

14. *Ex Parte Jepson*, 1971 Comm. Dec. 62 (Asst' Comm'r Pat. 1917).

15. *State Industries, Inc. v. Mor-Flo Industries, Inc.*, 883 F. 2d 1575 (Fed. Cir. 1989).

16. *Copyrights*, Title 17, U.S. CODE, §901.

17. *Rolls-Royce, Ltd. v. GTE Valeron Corp.*, 800 F. 2d 1101, 1110 n.9 (Fed. Cir. 1986).

18. *Patents*, Title 35, §102.

19. Ibid., §103. *Graham v. John Deer Co.*, 383 U.S. 1 (1960).

20. *Patents*, Title 35, §102(b).

21. *Westinghouse v. Boyden Brake*, 170 U.S. 537 (1898).

22. *Standard Oil Company v. American Cyanamid Company*, 774 F. 2d 448 (Fed. Cir. 1985).

23. *Patents*, Title 35, §102(b).

24. *Standard Oil v. American Cyanamid.*

25. *Patents*, Title 35, §251.

26. Ibid., §121.

27. *Graver Tank & Manufacturing Company v. Linde Air Products Company*, 339 U.S. 605 (1950).

28. *Copyrights*, Title 17, §901.

29. *Patents*, Title 35, §102.

30. *Copyrights*, Title 17, §412.

31. *Fitzgerald Publishing Co. v. Baylor Publishing Co.*, 807 F. 2d 1110 (2d Cir. 1986).

32. *Stix Products, Inc. v. United Merchants & Manufacturers, Inc.*, 295 F. Supp. 479 (S.D.N.Y. 1968).

33. *Patents*, Title 35, §271.

34. *Trademarks*, Title 15, §1125.

35. Ibid., §1127.

36. *Copyrights*, Title 17, §101.

# INDEX

# ESTABLISH A FRAMEWORK
# FOR EXCELLENCE
## WITH THE OASIS PRESS®

Fast-breaking changes in technology and the global marketplace continue to create unprecedented opportunities for businesses. However, with these opportunities come many new challenges. Today, more than ever, businesses — especially small businesses — need to excel in all areas of operation to compete and succeed in an ever-changing world.

*The Successful Business Library* helps you solve the day-to-day problems you face now, while preparing you for the unexpected problems you may be facing down the road. With any of our products, you will receive up-to-date and practical business solutions, which are easy to use and easy to understand. No jargon or theories, just solid, nuts-and-bolts information.

Whether you are an entrepreneur going into business for the first time or an experienced consultant trying to keep up with the latest rules and regulations, *The Successful Business Library* provides you with the step-by-step guidance, and action-oriented plans you need to succeed in today's world. As an added benefit, PSI Research/The Oasis Press® unconditionally guarantees your satisfaction with the purchase of any book in our catalog.

## www.oasispress.com

### More than a marketplace for our products, we actually provide something that many business Web sites tend to overlook ... useful information!

It's no mystery that the World Wide Web is a great way for businesses to promote their products; however, most commercial sites stop there. We have always viewed our site's goals a little differently. For starters, we have applied our 30 years of experience providing hands-on information to small businesses directly to our Web site. We offer current information to help you start your own business, guidelines to keep it up and running, useful federal and state-specific information (including addresses and phone numbers to contact these resources), and a forum for business owners to communicate and network with others on the Internet. We would like to invite you to check out our Web site and discover the information that can assist you and your small business venture.

# Don't Let Your Quest to Start Your Business Stop Yet!

## After all, your success is our success ...

**1** At PSI Research and The Oasis Press, we take pride in helping you and two million other businesses grow. We hope that we have helped you move toward a successful business start-up, but we also want you to know that we'll be here for you after you open your doors for business too.

On the following pages, we offer a brief sampling of The Successful Business Library — books and software that will help you solve your day-to-day issues and prepare you for unexpected problems your business may face down the road. We offer up-to-date and practical business solutions, which are easy to use and understand. Call for a complete catalog or let our knowledgeable sales representatives point you in the right direction.

## Committed to keeping you up-to-date ...

**2** Occasionally our fast-paced world doesn't allow us to get you the most current information in print until after you have already made an investment in one of our products. To solve this problem, we have created a resource on the Internet that can react to immediate changes in laws, regulations, and other business factors that could affect your business in the future. Our comprehensive website, www.oasispress.com, is designed to help you find the information you need. Just look for the link for *Start Your Business* or our *Business Solutions* for the most current contacts and updates.

### visit us at http://www.oasispress.com

## Your input means a lot to us ...

**3** Our doors are always open — whether it's to find out about a product that can assist you in building a smart, well-prepared business; to tell us about your business' own success story; or, to suggest ways we could improve our products for you — and we look forward to your call. For more information about our products or to request a complete catalog, call 1-800-228-2275. Our Web site also features a 24-hour online store to order any of our products, as well as a forms for comments and catalog requests.

# Successful Business Library

A Guide to Valuing a Small Business

## What's It Worth?

**by Lloyd R. Manning**

Determine what a business or investment is really worth. Whether buying or selling a business, this unique guide quickly shows readers how to get the best deal. Written without a lot of jargon, confusing discussions, or theoretical concepts, this book is ideal for anyone wanting to purchase a new business, to establish a fair selling price for a going business, or simply to have a better understanding of a professional appraiser's process.

With a friendly, hands-on approach, *What's It Worth?* will teach you:

- ❖ How real estate appraisers determine a fair market value for a business
- ❖ Why some specific appraisal methods and models should be preferred over others
- ❖ How to find a reasonable and appropriate price for a business

*What's It Worth?* informs readers how to avoid the most common pitfalls of buying a business: paying too much, buying a business that is on the decline or that is obsolete, or paying for good will that isn't all that good. Learn how to sort out what and why a person is selling, and how to accurately measure sales, profit, and good will.

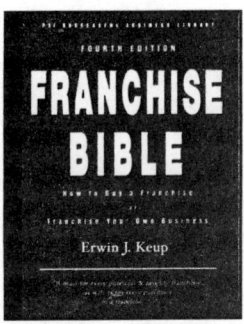

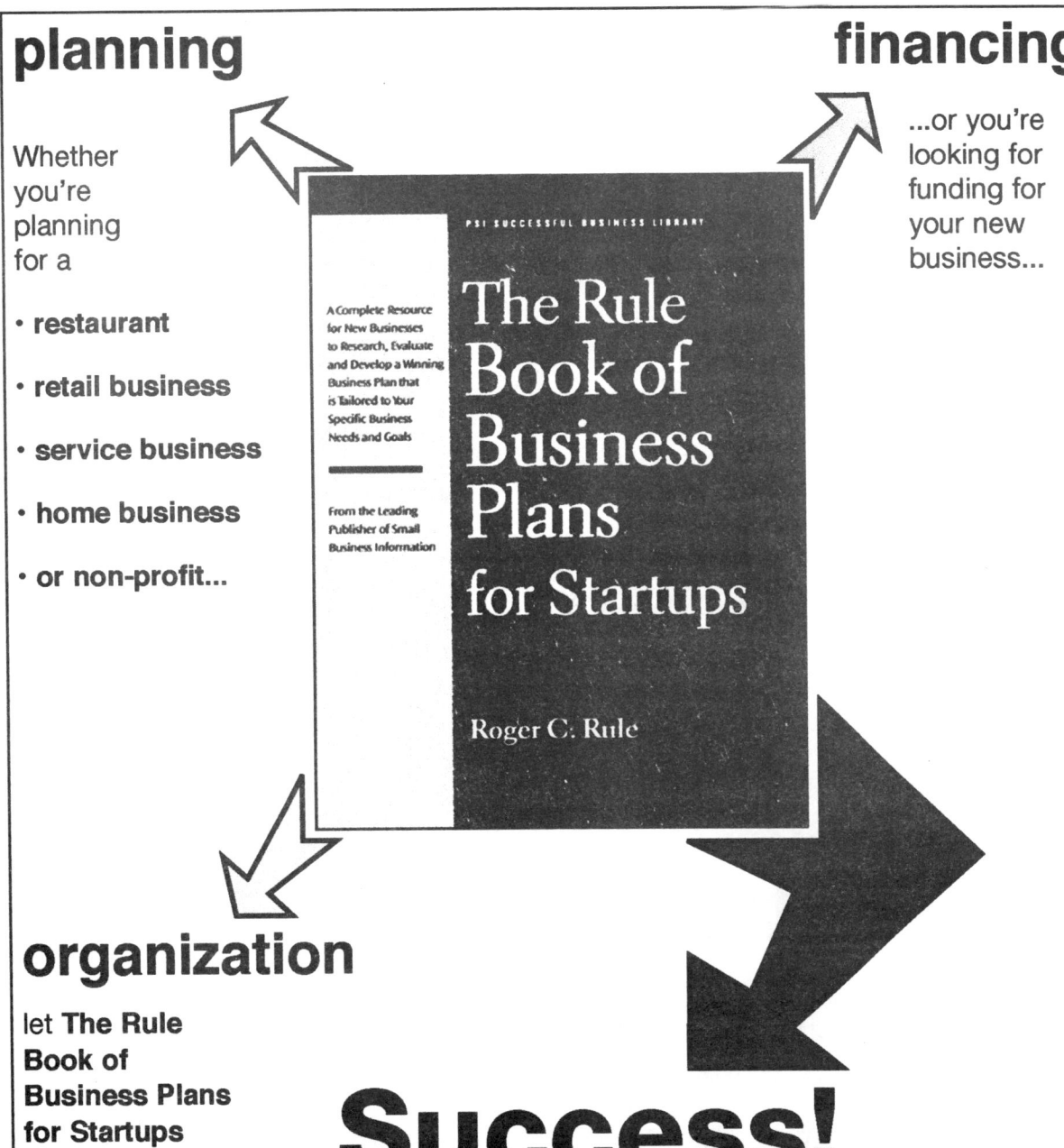

# Managing People
*A Practical Guide*

This action-oriented guide helps you increase efficiency and productivity by:

- ❖ Thinking Strategically
- ❖ Motivating Your Staff
- ❖ Working as a Team
- ❖ Evaluating Employees
- ❖ Setting Goals
- ❖ Delegating
- ❖ Coping with Stress
  — and more!

Managing People: A Practical Guide, 4th Edition
*Byron Lane*

217 pages          ISBN 1-55571-554-0          $21.95

# Truth about Teams
*A Facilitator's Survival Guide*

"Discover the power of teams. This is the best book I have ever seen to unleash the power of teams. The most comprehensive guide to making the change from the traditional autocratic leadership to self-directed teams."

— Mike Oxley, Manager of Quality Assurance
Borg-Warner Automotive

Truth About Teams: A Facilitator's Survival Guide
*J.T. Houston, Ed.D.*

152 pages          ISBN 1-55571-482-X          $18.95

# A Company Policy & Personnel Workbook

*A Company Policy and Personnel Workbook* is a practical, easy-to-use guide that provides your business with a direct approach for developing a company personnel manual. It explains topics such as employee safety, leave of absence, flex time, smoking, substance abuse, sexual harassment, job performance, and Internet use.

Includes 80 model policies and 28 ready-to-use personnel forms.

| A Company Policy & Personnel Workbook |
| :---: |
| *Ardella Ramey & Carl R.J. Sniffen* |

| 336 pages | ISBN 1-55571-486-2 | $29.95 |
| --- | --- | --- |

# Improving Staff Productivity

By following the easy-to-implement techniques, you can expect to potentially generate significant time and money savings and improve your overall operations and custom service.

| Improving Staff Productivity |
| :---: |
| *Ben Harrison Carter* |

| 113 pages | ISBN 1-55571-456-0 | $16.95 |
| --- | --- | --- |